Tasty Treats for
DemanDing DogS

Gregg R. Gillespie

Main Street
A division of Sterling Publishing Co., Inc.
New York

The Library of Congress has cataloged the previous edition as follows:

Gillespie, Gregg R., 1934-
Tasty treats for demanding dogs / Gregg R. Gillespie.
 p. cm.
ISBN 0-8069-4562-1
 1. Dogs-Food-Recipes. I. Title

SF427. 4. G55 2001
639.7'0855—dc21   2002031434

10 9 8 7 6 5 4 3

Published by Sterling Publishing Co., Inc.
387 Park Avenue South, New York, NY 10016
© 2001 by Gregg R. Gillespie
Distributed in the United Kingdom by GMC Distribution Services,
Castle Place, 166 High Street, Lewes, East Sussex, England BN7 1XU
Printed in China
All rights reserved

Edited by Jeanette Green
Designed by Richard Oriolo

Sterling ISBN-13: 978-1-4027-3179-2
      ISBN-10: 1-4027-3179-5

For information about custom editions, special sales, premium and
corporate purchases, please contact Sterling Special Sales
Department at 800-805-5489 or specialsales@sterlingpub.com.

Contents

Introduction — 7

   How I Got Started — 7

The Care & Feeding of Your Best Friend — 11

   Chef's Secrets — 13

Choosing Ingredients & Substitutions — 15

   Dry Ingredients — 15

   Processed Foods — 21

   Natural Products — 22

   Meat Products — 23

Owner's Alert: What Not to Feed Your Dog — 27

   Dogs Are Individuals — 30

   Foods to Avoid — 31

LIP-SMACKING RECIPES — 33

Index of Doggy Treats — 127

Acknowledgments

I would be remiss if I didn't thank the thousands of owners who have fed their dogs my treats. My dog cookies, sold under the trademark Dobis, have been consumed worldwide. I am also grateful to the animal-control officers and attendants in Reno, Nevada, for their enthusiasm when I dropped off bags of cookies at the shelter. I had to quickly add, "Hey guys, wait! These cookies aren't for you to eat. They're for the dogs!"

Next on my list is the Washoe County Humane Society. The director and staff were unstinting in allowing me free access to their facilities when I was testing various cookies and treats. My only wish was that I might have been able to take all the dogs home with me.

My final acknowledgment is to all the wonderful dogs I've owned and lived with since 1970. Each loving dog had its own personality and gave me so much more than it got. Of these eight dogs, I must give special recognition to Nefer-Temu, who launched my search for a better dog treat. And I cannot forget Abu, the greatest friend I have ever had in my life.

INTRODUCTION

How I Got Started

For more years than I'd care to admit, I've been preparing both food and treats for my dogs. It began when I was young and could barely afford food for myself. Of course, before I could think of my needs, I had to consider what I could feed Nefer-Temu, a one-year-old Basenji.

I never realized what I was taking on. I found out that I couldn't simply go out into the kitchen and prepare something. That would be a waste of money—and I was in no position to waste money.

I also needed to find out what dogs really would or could eat. My first stop was at my local veterinarian's. I learned that a dog is a carnivore, and while I thought I knew this already, I had no idea what it meant in terms of canine nutrition. Simply put, it means that dogs eat meat; dogs depend on meat as an essential feature of their diet.

That means that I would have to try to give Nefer the same healthful diet he would find for himself in the wild, a diet that would not include corn and mush or beans and rice. Although this fact is well known, a recent dog-cookie book stated that dogs are omnivores—they'll eat meat, vegetables, and all kinds of things. Yes, dogs eat other things besides meat—mainly prepared foods we have taught them to eat. And yes, they nibble on grass, eat cheese, drink milk, and, no thanks to college fraternity guys, they may even drink beer. Fact: Pampered pets may eagerly eat candy, even chocolate, almost anything over-flavored with spices. Fortunately, these dietary extravagances are the exception, not the rule.

To repeat, dogs are primarily meat-eaters, and when you're preparing dog food at home, you need to keep that in mind. Beef, lamb, pork, or poultry innards—the heart, liver, and kidneys—make a nutritious meal for dogs. It's OK to exclude the entrails, but remember that the heart is one of the most fat-free organ meats, and indeed, one of the most fat-free meats available.

Most people forget that a dog smells before it eats, and it is only after the food clears his mouth that he tastes it. While innards and entrails do not smell appetizing to humans, dogs in the wild would fight or even kill for the opportunity to eat them.

With all this information, I returned to my kitchen and worked for days to create my first dog treat. These treats were a success—not only with my dog, but with every dog in the neighborhood. What had begun in my kitchen resulted in my traveling 3,200 miles coast-to-coast to establish my first dog-cookie factory. It opened in 1977 in Portsmouth, New Hampshire, and was finally relocated to a large two-story complex in Rochester, New Hampshire.

In going commercial with my dog cookies and my ideas, I soon learned about government regulations, acceptable nutritional levels for labeling a product as affording dogs "complete nutrition." As it turned out, the cookies I had first produced were less than .0018 percent away from being qualified for such labeling. So I increased the nutritional value of my recipes, and my cookies were soon sold around the world, even becoming favorites of award-winning show dogs and racers.

In 1983 I left the dog-cookie business. Since that time I have never stopped preparing and trying to improve the treats I feed my dogs as well as the beloved pets of friends and relatives.

Through the years I have talked with hundreds of dog lovers, pet-shop owners, and others dedicated to the well-being of pets and other animals. I've discovered many pets that live on restricted diets. I've learned that, like human beings, dogs have certain medical conditions and allergies that may cause physical problems. I've offered dog owners the dietary information I've collected.

I've created all the recipes in this book, modifying a few from older existing recipes and carefully excluding any ingredients that could be harmful to dogs. In my factory office, I hung a sign: "I will not put anything into your dog that I would not put into my child." May your dog enjoy these treats in good health!

—GREGG R. GILLESPIE

The Care & Feeding of Your

Best Friend

Most chefs who write cookbooks for dogs emphasize the taste and appearance of the finished dish but neglect nutrition and how the food smells. When creating recipes for dogs, scent is all-important and nutrition essential. If the dog treats fail to appeal to your dog's nose, they may be left in the bowl uneaten. If they fail to offer adequate nutrition, your dog may not maintain optimal health.

In the end, solid nutrition must be the primary standard, with smell and taste, often called palatability, secondary. Of the half-dozen dog-food-related cookbooks in print, many are filled with recipes rather easily recognized as coming from cookbooks written for people. Still other dog-food cookbooks would not be out of place on a shelf of comics or cartoon books.

Feeding a dog, or any animal, is serious business; it should not be taken lightly.

Many dog-food cookbooks contain ingredients that should not be fed to all dogs. Notes need to be included about foods specific dog breeds cannot eat.

In one of these books I found a recipe for so-called party snacks for dogs. Ingredients included: chicken liver, onions, mustard, brandy, orange juice, nutmeg, and cream. At least two of these ingredients (onions and brandy) should not be fed to dogs.

Yet another cartoon cookbook offers a recipe for barbecue sauce. Its ingredients include: green peppers, garlic, tomato sauce, Worcestershire sauce, ketchup, brown sugar, red wine vinegar, onions, and water. You and I might like the sauce, but a dog would not.

This recipe, like the chicken-liver recipe, contains onions. Although most humans love onions, onions can be deadly to a few dog breeds. The Akita and Shiba breeds are extremely sensitive to onions, which make them more susceptible to Heinz body anemia. This physical disorder can weaken them and contribute to their death.

For untold centuries, dogs have been humans' faithful companions. Although both dogs and humans eat meat, the omnivorous human diet has had an influence, for good or ill, on the diet of domestic dogs. They have shared both meat and meal. Although canines are primarily meat-eaters, they have changed their habits in more recent centuries to suit those of their owners. Dogs have adapted to their two-legged friends.

No animal will starve itself to death without good reason. If you place a plate of meat before a dog, the scraps will be eagerly consumed. If you offer the dog a plate of vegetables, the same dog will turn away. However, if you offer a dog a plate of vegetables day after day, the dog will continue to refuse them until he gets hungry; only then will he consume them. The reason is simple: the dog became so hungry that he would eat almost anything. After living on the vegetable diet for a while, the dog will eventually refuse a plate of meat, just as he had once refused vegetables.

For years, veterinarians and dog breeders have used this method of switching diets. This method is also commonly used to alter the diet of other animals.

The key to keeping a dog healthy is proper food in healthful proportions. An approved diet can include dog cookies, biscuits, and treats. However, you should not feed dogs cookies, biscuits, and treats made for humans. Two common ingredients in human cookies are processed sugar and chocolate, which are not recommended for dogs.

Also, most people are not aware that chocolate contains arsenic. It is in a natural form and has little or no effect on the human body. But the metabolism of a dog, especially that of smaller breeds, is different from that of a human. Dogs are sensitive to arsenic. Even in small quantities arsenic could be deadly—not that it will, but it could be.

Small quantities of arsenic are also present in certain vegetables like kohlrabi, turnips, certain cereals, apple seeds, sea fish, sea salt, milk, and egg yolk. Arsenic in minute doses is present in the human thyroid gland, thymus gland, mammary gland, head, and hair.

Although its nutritional needs differ, do not feed your dog anything you would not feed your child. Avoid additives, unnatural foods, and fillers.

Chef's Secrets

How do you preserve the dog cookies after they have been baked? For the past 25 years, I have used this simple and successful process: Bake the cookies or treats according to the directions for each recipe. When all the cookies are baked, cool them slightly. Then pile all of them back onto a single baking sheet or tray. Return the tray to the oven (with the heat turned off) for a period not less than 8 hours. The cookies must remain undisturbed—without opening the oven door—for that period of time. This drying time will remove a good deal of moisture still present in the treats. Afterward you can store the cookies or treats at room temperature in a regular paper bag or a container that isn't airtight. The dog treats will contain little moisture, which greatly reduces the chance of mold forming.

The primary cookie ingredient is whole-wheat flour. I prefer to use whole-wheat flour for dusting the flat surface used for rolling out the dough as well.

If you have added too much liquid, you may need to add 1 tablespoon or more of flour. Do not add anything extra except flour.

Most dog-cookie manufacturers rarely mention that any wheat-based product may attract moths if stored in a dark place undisturbed for long periods of time. It's best to keep these dog cookies out in the open. Most dogs enjoy a crunchy treat, and dry cookies will help keep their teeth clean.

Nearly all the recipes in this book are for dog cookies or snacks. That's because they're dry and crunchy like a cracker. I've found that a dry treat has the longest shelf life. The terms *cookie, biscuit,* and *treat* are used roughly interchangeably. (I wanted to have fun with recipe titles; you get tired of chewing on the same old cookie.) You can use standard small cookie cutters for most of them, but you might want to be more inventive, creating dog bones and other shapes. I do include a couple recipes for softer breads. These should be kept refrigerated.

Please note that all recipe yields are approximate. They depend on many factors, such as how thick you roll out the dough, the fullness of the teaspoon, and more. Of course, experienced cooks know this. Also remember that you'll want to make very small cookies if you have a very small dog. Watch the puppy or dog eating to make sure your pet can handle the size of cookie you feed him.

I sometimes use a sausage-making attachment to my mixer to make round dog cookies. The process is simple. Make the dough according to directions, and being sure the dough is not too dry, process it through the sausage-maker into long round pieces. Then cut the rounds into desired sizes. This way, you can make long ones for large dogs and tiny ones for small dogs.

Many of these cookies require beef, chicken, or lamb broth. Although you can substitute bouillon cubes for the desired broth, it's best to use the real thing. I think bouillon cubes are preferable to cans of bouillon soup. However, most bouillon cubes on the market contain chemicals, specifically monosodium glutamate (MSG), sometimes disguised in the product ingredient list by the catch phrase "natural flavors." At all costs, I avoid ingesting this substance and would not consider buying this salt product for my dogs either. MSG is not a desirable additive.

Choosing the Best Ingredients & Substitutions

 If you want your cookies to turn out just right, it's best to choose great ingredients. Your dog will thank you.

Dry Ingredients

All-Purpose Flour All-purpose flour is a processed flour that can be either bleached or unbleached. In these recipes, all-purpose flour can be used interchangeably with whole-wheat flour. Do not substitute all-purpose flour for self-rising flour. Of course, whole-wheat flour is preferred. It is more nutritious and fewer chemicals are used in processing whole-wheat flour.

Baking Powder This leavening ingredient is a mixture of baking soda, cornstarch, and cream of tartar. Both double-acting and single-acting varieties are available.

Baking Soda Known as bicarbonate of soda, this product is used for leavening baked goods. When combined with acidic products, baking soda releases gas bubbles that make dough rise. Always add baking soda with other dry ingredients, and add it before adding liquid to the dry ingredients.

Bisquick® or Biscuit Mix Bisquick is the brand name of an all-purpose baking mix. You can use any dry commercial biscuit mix as a substitute.

Bone Meal This flourlike substance consists of ground-up bones of cattle. It adds calcium, phosphorus, and other trace minerals to the dog's diet. Current concerns about scrapie and BSE mean that you need to choose the product carefully. Find nutritional bone meal in a health-food store.

Brewer's Yeast This is a special yeast rich in B-complex vitamins. It cannot be used as a leavening agent. Nutritional yeast, found in many health-food stores, may be used as a substitute.

Buckwheat Flour Buckwheat flour is made from crushed herbs of the genus *Fagopyrum*. In these recipes, there is no substitute for this flour.

Bulgur Wheat Bulgur wheat consists of whole-wheat grains without the bran that have been partially steamed then ground. Cracked wheat may be used as a substitute.

Corn-Muffin Mix or Cornbread Mix These dry commercial products allow easy preparation of corn muffins or cornbread. There is no substitute.

Cracked Wheat This fine-grained product is made by crushing the wheat berry (grain) into smaller fragments. Cracked wheat requires less liquid and a shorter cooking time than whole wheat. Bulgur wheat can be a substitute for cracked wheat.

Desiccated Beef-Liver Powder Desiccated beef-liver powder may be the single most important ingredient used in dog cookies and treats. This commercial product is made from beef liver that has been dried and reduced to a powder. A single pound of dried beef-liver powder is equal to about 10 pounds of beef liver. Raw liver could be substituted for this powder, but the recipe would have to be adjusted for the difference in moisture. Look for desiccated beef-liver powder at a health-food store. You can substitute desiccated pork liver, which reportedly has a higher nutritional content than beef liver. *If you have difficulty finding desiccated beef liver, you can order the product: P.O. Box 4884, Springfield, Missouri 65808; (417) 890-8636; or on the web at www.leviticus11.com*

Garlic Powder This powdery substance is made from dried ground garlic flakes. Finely crushed garlic cloves can substitute for this product. Do not use garlic powder with additives.

> **PLEASE NOTE:** *Some dogs may be allergic to garlic or garlic powder. Do not use spoiled garlic cloves.*

Gelatin Gelatin (also called gelatine) is an odorless, tasteless, and colorless thickening agent. This protein substance is extracted from bone or certain kinds of seaweed, like agar-agar or alginates. It's available as a powder or in translucent sheets. It is usually dissolved in warm water. In these recipes, it creates glazes that are brushed on baked goods. There is no substitute for gelatin.

Graham Flour Graham flour, named after a nutritionist, usually contains flakes of wheat bran ground in varying degrees of coarseness. The germ is commonly removed to prolong its shelf life. This wheat flour is slightly coarser and sweeter than regular whole-wheat flour. A coarse whole-wheat flour would be the only substitute.

Kelp Powder *Kelp* is a generic name for all edible seaweeds. Finely chopped dried parsley can be used as a substitute, but the cookies or biscuits would have a different vitamin and mineral content.

Kibble Dog Food *Kibble* refers to coarsely ground meal or grain, commonly used in dry dog food. You can use any kind of dry dog food in these recipes.

Oat Bran Oat bran is the outer casing of the oats, which has a high fiber content. Wheat bran can be used as a substitute.

Oatmeal or Rolled Oats The rolled oats used in these recipes are sometimes referred to as old-fashioned oatmeal. You may use the quick- or slow-cooking varieties. However, do not use instant oatmeal packets; they contain ingredients other than oatmeal. The added ingredients might not blend well with other recipe ingredients.

Pumpkin Seeds Dry pumpkin seeds are a good source of magnesium, iron, phosphorus, zinc, copper, potassium, niacin, and folic acid. They add crunch and a pleasant texture to a cookie. Use them raw or roasted, but commercially roasted seeds may contain salt and oil.

Rice Flour Glutinous or sweet rice flour is a sweet flour or powder made from short-grain rice that becomes moist, firm, and sticky when cooked. This is because it contains a higher proportion of waxy starch molecules than medium- or long-grain rice. Because of its chewy texture, glutinous rice flour is a favorite base for dumplings, buns, and pastries. Sweets made with glutinous rice flour are popular in Southeast Asia. There is no substitution for rice flour.

Rye Flour Rye flour is a heavy, dark, low-gluten flour milled from a cereal grass. Any of the four available varieties can be used in these recipes. The varieties are light, medium, dark, and pumpernickel. There is no substitute for rye flour.

Sesame Seeds These small, flavorful seeds, also known as benné seeds, are used extensively in cooking throughout the world. Sesame seeds can be used fresh or toasted. There is no substitution.

Soy flour Soy flour, or kinako, is a finely ground flour made from soybeans that has twice the protein value of whole-wheat flour. Soy flour is rarely used alone; generally it is used with other flours. Soy flour does not have gluten, so it does not rise. White corn flour has the same texture and could serve as a substitute. The taste of the finished cookie or biscuit, however, would differ.

Sunflower Seeds Sunflower seeds, with hulls removed, are rich in protein and fat. Use the raw seeds in these recipes. Roasted sunflower seeds may contain salt, oil, and other additives. Hulled pumpkin seeds make a reasonable substitute.

Textured Vegetable Protein (TVP) TVP is a gritty substance made from soybeans that's used to increase the nutritional value of a recipe. There is no substitute.

Turbinado Sugar Turbinado sugar is raw sugar that has been steam-cleaned. Standard white sugar cannot be used as a substitute.

Wheat Bran Wheat bran is the outer layer of the wheat kernel removed during the milling process. At one time, the bran was discarded; today it enjoys various advantages in the baking process. It is an excellent source of protein, vitamins, and minerals. Oat bran can be a substitute for wheat bran.

Wheat Flakes Wheat flakes are produced the same way that rolled oats are produced. They must be soaked for several hours before they are cooked. The nutritional value of the flakes varies with the refining process.

Wheat Germ Wheat germ is the small flakes obtained from crushing the germ of the wheat berry, which is rich in protein, minerals, and vitamins. When added to foods, wheat germ increases nutritional value. It must be kept refrigerated since it can become rancid quickly. There is no substitute.

White Corn Flour White corn flour is made from finely ground cornmeal obtained from dry corn kernels. Corn flour has a low gluten content and must be combined with wheat flour to produce leavening. It cannot be used interchangeably with yellow cornmeal in a recipe.

Do not confuse corn flour with cornstarch (which is sometimes called cornflour), used for thickening puddings. Cornstarch is obtained from extracting the starch from the endosperm of the corn kernel.

Whole-Wheat Flour Whole-wheat flour is produced by milling the entire wheat grain. Cookies and biscuits made with whole-wheat instead of white flour are more nutritious, tend to be darker, and have a stronger flavor and less volume. If you want lighter baked goods, sift the whole-wheat flour several times before using it. Store it in the refrigerator. Unbleached all-purpose flour can serve as a less nutritious substitute.

Yellow Cornmeal Yellow cornmeal is a semolina or coarse meal obtained from grinding dried corn kernels. Polenta can be used as a substitute; do not use white cornmeal as a substitute. White cornmeal flour undergoes a different milling process. White and yellow cornmeal are not interchangeable in a recipe.

Dairy Products & Eggs

Butter This dairy product is produced by churning cream. Most commercial butter is made from cow's milk, but it can also be churned from the milk of other mammals, such as goats, buffalo, or camels. Butter cannot be heated at high temperatures since it burns. It contains high levels of fat, saturated fatty acids, and cholesterol. The butter used in these recipes is from cow's milk.

Cheddar Cheese Cheddar cheese is a semi-firm, uncooked, pressed cheese ripened for a relatively long period under cool and very humid conditions. The cheese should not be dry or crumbly and the outer part should not be darker than the inner part. Any semi-firm cheese, such as Gouda, Edam, fontina, or Monterey Jack, can be used as a substitute.

Cottage Cheese This fresh cheese made from pasteurized cow's milk is not ripened or fermented. Cottage cheese has a short shelf life. Like other fresh cheeses, it can contain up to 80% water and is low in fat and calories. It may have a slightly acidic taste. Cottage cheese is available in small-curd, medium-curd, and large-curd. Any fresh cheese, such as ricotta, mascarpone, cream cheese, or Petit-Suisse, can be used as a substitute.

Eggs Eggs have a high protein content and are packed with nutrition. The color of the shell depends on the hen's breed and has no reflection on the nutritional value of the egg. Unless otherwise stated, use fresh large hen's eggs. Although humans need to wash everything that touches raw eggs (or chickens) in hot soapy water to protect them against salmonella bacteria, this is less of a concern for dogs.

Milk These recipes use whole fresh cow's milk. Goat's milk may be substituted; we have not tested soy milk in these recipes. You might want to try it.

Nonfat Dry Milk Nonfat dry milk is a dairy product that has had all of its fat and moisture removed. This powdered milk is also known as nonfat dried skim milk, or dried skim milk. Fresh skim milk would be the only substitute, but the recipe's moisture content would have to be adjusted to compensate for the additional liquid.

Parmesan Cheese This hard dry cheese has a granular texture. Parmesan cheese can be grated and used to flavor many foods. You can substitute Romano cheese or any hard cheese that can be grated. Avoid dried out, bulging, or pasty cheeses.

Romano Cheese Grate this hard dry Italian cheese just as you would Parmesan cheese. Most firm, hard cheeses have been cooked or pressed.

Yogurt Yogurt is produced when lactic bacteria is added to milk, which ferments. It is a good source of calcium. The fat, carbohydrate, and calorie contents of commercial yogurts vary greatly.

Processed Foods

Canola Oil Canola oil, the commercial name for rapeseed oil, contains just 6% saturated fat, the lowest of any oil. When heated to high temperatures it may have an unpleasant odor. Corn oil and safflower oil, which are not as low in saturated fat, may be used as substitutes.

Carob Chips These chocolate-style chips, used just as you would chocolate chips, are made from carob. This product has been considered safe for dogs allergic to chocolate.

Corn Oil Corn oil is a good nutritional source of fat for dogs. It's rich in polyunsaturated fats and contains fatty acids, which help fight cholesterol. Canola oil can be a substitute; check for allergies.

CAUTION: *Many dogs, like many people, may be allergic to corn-based products, such as corn oil. This may be because of its ubiquitous use in foodstuffs.*

Meat-Flavored Baby Food Commercial baby-food products containing meat and sold in small jars are widely available. Choose from a variety of brand names; there is no substitution for this product.

PLEASE NOTE: *Some baby foods contain monosodium glutamate (MSG).*

Molasses Molasses is a by-product of cane-sugar refining. Blackstrap molasses, a dark, strong-tasting, slightly sweet liquid, is the product of the third and final extraction and contains more nutrients than sorghum, a lighter molasses. The terms *sulfured* and *unsulfured* indicate whether sulfur was used during refining. For these recipes, use only unsulfured molasses. This product is also known as treacle.

Peanut Butter Peanut butter is the paste made from crushing or grinding raw peanuts. (Peanuts are actually legumes, not nuts.) This nutritious food is rich in protein, fat, and calories. It is an excellent source of thiamine, niacin, magnesium, and potassium. Do not substitute another nut butter for this product. Use only the smooth variety in these recipes.

Safflower Oil This oil is extracted from cartham seeds. The unrefined oil (amber color) has a sweet hazelnut flavor, and the refined version (very pale yellow) has a more neutral flavor. Safflower oil, low in saturated fat, oxidizes quickly.

Vegetable Shortening Vegetable shortening is a solid fat made from vegetable oils. Lard or chilled pork fat can be used as a substitute. The process of hydrogenation converts unsaturated fats into saturated fats.

Natural Products

Carrots Use fresh, not canned, carrots in these recipes. This root vegetable, rich in vitamin A and potassium, should be washed or gently scraped. Only old carrots need to be peeled. There is no substitute for carrots in these recipes.

Garlic Use crushed fresh garlic for these recipes unless garlic powder is specified. Do not use spoiled garlic. Garlic must be cooked for a dog to be able to digest it. This herb is used extensively in human cuisines, but it is less common in dog recipes.

PLEASE NOTE: *Some individual dogs may be allergic to garlic or garlic powder. Do not use spoiled garlic cloves. Also, some dog breeds may be intolerant of garlic. Onions can be used as a substitute, but note that a few dog breeds may not tolerate onions either. The Akita and Shiba breeds are extremely sensitive to onions and should not eat them.*

Honey Honey is a sweet substance that bees make from flower nectar. Usually bees gather a single type of nectar, which produces a honey with a distinctive flavor. Honey can be liquid or crystallized. These recipes use the liquid; there is no substitute for honey.

Parsley The parsley used in these recipes is the fresh, snipped herb, not the dried, crumbled commercial product.

Peas & Corn For peas and corn you can use a frozen mixture of the vegetables.

Meat Products

Of course, you need to be cautious about the source of your meats and meat products. It's even more important today because hoof-and-mouth disease and scrapie (BSE), which have infected livestock in Europe, could easily spread to other parts of the world.

Bacon & Bacon Drippings Bacon comes from cured and sometimes smoked pork. Sliced bacon is usually produced from pork bellies and back bacon from loins. Use ordinary American bacon, or, if desired, the meatier Canadian bacon. Bacon drippings are the fat produced when pork is cooked. Bacon is high in fat and sodium.

Warning: Commercial bacon sold in supermarkets may contain MSG, nitrates, and other chemicals. If bacon drippings are used, the residue of these nonfat additives may be present. Cooking bacon at high heat speeds up the formation of nitrosamines, thought to be carcinogenic.

Beef, Beef Broth & Beef Drippings The meat of a cow. Choose the cut specified in the recipe; otherwise, it is what your budget allows. Beef broth is the liquid in which beef has been cooked, whether alone or accompanied by vegetables and other ingredients. The often fatty drippings are the residue collected in the bottom of a pan in which beef has been cooked.

Beef Bouillon Beef bouillon, sometimes called beef broth, is the liquid resulting from cooking beef. Commercial bouillon is available as a liquid, a powder, or cubes.

Usually commercial beef bouillon contains a high amount of sodium and may contain monosodium glutamate (MSG), which is not good for dogs.

Chicken, Chicken Broth & Chicken Drippings Chickens are the offspring, over 4 months old, of hens. Many people prefer free-range chickens, which are allowed outside rather than being confined to a chicken coop. Since all chickens are killed when very young, the meat stands up well when cooked with dry heat. Chicken meat contains less fat than red and white meats, but it has an equal amount of cholesterol if the skin is eaten.

Chicken broth is the liquid in which chicken has been cooked, either alone or accompanied by vegetables. Chicken drippings are usually considered the residue remaining in the bottom of a pan in which chicken has been cooked.

Chicken Bouillon Chicken bouillon, or chicken broth, is obtained from cooking chicken. It is available as a liquid, a powder, or cubes. Commercial bouillon may contain a high amount of sodium and may contain monosodium glutamate (MSG), which is not good for dogs.

Frankfurters & Sausages Frankfurters (franks) and sausages are made from pork or beef. A wide variety of sausages, such as kielbasa, lap cheong, merguez, mortadella, salami, weisswurst, bratwurst, pepperoni, and chorizo, are available. Favor sausage with the fewest additives and spices.

Warning: Most sausage-type products contain MSG, nitrates, or other chemical additives.

Lamb & Lamb Drippings Lamb or mutton is the meat of a sheep. The drippings are usually considered the residue remaining in the bottom of a pan in which lamb has been cooked.

Pork & Pork Drippings Pork is the meat of a pig. The drippings are usually considered the residue remaining in the bottom of a pan in which pork has been cooked. These drippings will usually have a high fat content, which must be considered when using them in a given recipe.

Salt pork and its drippings are used as a flavoring agent. Salt pork is usually discarded after cooking, leaving the drippings.

Turkey & Turkey Drippings Turkey is a very large, meaty bird with dark and light meat. Prefer whole turkey to smoked turkey or boneless turkey, which may be over-processed and contain undesirable additives. Domestic varieties are probably preferable to wild turkeys. Turkey drippings are the liquid and fat that remain in the bottom of the pan after a turkey has been roasted.

Metric Equivalents

Liquid or Capacity Measures

1 quart = 4 cups = 960 milliliters = 32 fluid ounces
1 pint = 2 cups = 480 milliliters = 16 fluid ounces
$1^3/_4$ cups = 420 milliliters = 14 fluid ounces
$1^1/_2$ cups = 360 milliliters = 12 fluid ounces
$1^1/_4$ cups = 300 milliliters = 10 fluid ounces
1 cup = 240 milliliters = $^1/_2$ pint = 8 fluid ounces
$^3/_4$ cup = 180 milliliters = 6 fluid ounces
$^1/_2$ cup = 120 milliliters = 4 fluid ounces
$^1/_3$ cup = 80 milliliters = 2.6 fluid ounces
$^1/_4$ cup = 60 milliliters = 2 fluid ounces
$^1/_8$ cup = 30 milliliters = 1 fluid ounce

Tablespoons & Teaspoons

2 Tablespoons = $^1/_8$ cup = 30 milliliters = 1 fluid ounce
1 Tablespoon = 3 teaspoons = 15 milliliters
1 teaspoon = 5 milliliters
$^3/_4$ teaspoon = 4 milliliters (3.75 milliliters)
$^1/_2$ teaspoon = 2.5 milliliters
$^1/_4$ teaspoon = 1 milliliter (1.25 milliliters)
$^1/_8$ teaspoon = 0.5 milliliter = pinch
dash = less than a pinch or $^1/_{16}$ teaspoon

Weight

2.2 pound = 1 kilogram
2 pounds = 900 grams or 0.9 kilogram (908 grams)
$1^1/_2$ pound = 675 grams (681 grams)
1 pound = 16 ounces = 450 grams (454 grams)
8 ounces = $^1/_2$ pound = 225 grams (227 grams)
4 ounces = $^1/_4$ pound = 110 grams (112 grams)
1 ounce = 30 grams (28 grams)
$^1/_2$ ounce = 15 grams (14 grams)

Length

1 inch = 2.5 centimeters (2.54 centimeters)
$^1/_2$ inch = 1.25 centimeters

Temperature

To convert Centigrade (Celsius) to Fahrenheit degrees, use this formula:
$^9/_5$ °C + 32 = °F
To convert Fahrenheit to Centigrade (Celsius) degrees, use this formula:
$^5/_9$ (°F - 32) = °C

Owner's Alert: What Not to Feed Your dog

People who buy pet treats rarely examine the label or ask how the ingredients might affect their dog's health. They never ask or consider: Are we transferring many of our human allergies to our pets by what we feed them? Then add the toxic products in our homes and the additives in our food, and the list of what not to feed your dog lengthens and demands serious concern.

Here are a few simple rules for feeding your dog. When buying food, buy the best you can afford, and remember that price does not always indicate the best food available. Always have clean, fresh water available. Remember: When feeding a pet, cute does not exist. Seeing a dog drink from a half-full margarita glass on the coffee table is not cute but stupid. It can kill!

Raw Foods Fad: The recent trend in feeding dogs raw meat, similar to what they would eat in the wild, may introduce diseases that are normally killed by cooking. People, of course, need to take particular care in handling any uncooked ingredients. Even dried grains might be coated with pesticides. Remember to wash with hot soapy water everything that raw meat, poultry, or uncooked eggs touch.

Salmonella: This is a bacteria found in chicken, eggs, and other poultry products. While salmonella can be dangerous for humans, it is not usually considered unsafe to dogs. For the safety of you and your family, always cook the bird or eggs through and thoroughly wash any kitchen surfaces they touch.

Nightshade Family Plants & Vegetables: Avoid any plants or plant material that could contain alkaloids such as scopolamine (hyoscine), atropine, or other neurotoxins that could cause nerve damage, paralysis, arthritislike symptoms, or even death. These are usually found in nightshade family vegetables like tomatoes, peppers, white potatoes, eggplant, and zucchini. Remember that seasonings, like cayenne pepper and paprika, and capsaicin contain these chemicals as well. Home-grown potato leaves can contain solanine, which may trouble domesticated animals. (These foods may also cause arthritislike symptoms in vulnerable humans.)

Of course, you want to avoid belladonna (deadly nightshade) as well as the nightshade plants love apple and horse nettle. Also avoid garden leaves and greens, like potato, rhubarb, and tomato leaves, which are toxic for dogs.

Garden: Outdoor garden and lawn fertilizers and chemicals, such as nitrogen, could also be harmful to some dogs. Dogs will be attracted to the smell of bone meal, blood meal, and fish emulsions. The best rule for dealing with these chemicals that could adversely affect dogs is to not allow your pets near the treated area for at least 24 hours after their use.

Flowers: In your flower bed, take great care that your dog does not touch these flowers, since they could cause ill effects: bittersweet (nightshade), buttercups, daffodils, delphiniums, foxgloves, lupine (Texas bluebonnet), morning glories, periwinkle, wisteria, azaleas, rhododendrons, hibiscus, oleander, and lilies of the valley. Although daffodil flowers and leaves may not cause problems, the bulb is considered dangerous.

Indoor Houseplants: Some indoor houseplants could adversely affect a dog; the list is endless. Be extremely careful if you grow these plants: aloe vera, dieffenbachia, dracaena, asparagus ferns, rubber plants, schefflera, and poinsettia.

Fruit Pits, Stones & Kernels: Don't let kernels and pits from fresh fruits fall into a spot where your dog might chew on them. Many pits contain small amounts of cyanide or arsenic. Avoid letting a dog near cherry, apricot, and peach pits.

Almonds & Castor Beans: Castor beans can be fatal for a dog that chews them. Avoid feeding dogs almonds.

Chocolate: Whether to feed a dog chocolate has been a controversial topic. Some people feel that the only side effect of this food is its addictive aspect or caffeinelike effects. Most chocolate products consumed by humans contain sugar, and the sugar can cause diabetes. Since chocolate contains arsenic (as do the foods kohlrabi, turnips, certain cereals, apple seeds, sea fish, sea salt, milk, and egg yolk in minute amounts), the toxic chemical could be harmful and cause damage or even death. Recipes in this book use carob in place of chocolate.

Caffeine: Caffeine, found in coffee, tea, and soft drinks, can be toxic to some dogs. Also, dogs may become addicted to the caffeine and sugar in many drinks. Dogs may also be afflicted with diabetes.

Processed Sugar: Processed sugar can cause diabetes in dogs. Processed sugar includes granulated sugar, powdered sugar, and brown sugar; do not use them when feeding your dog. Take particular care that processed sugar is not contained in food you purchase.

Garlic & Onions: Although garlic and onions are used in many dog treats, individual dogs may not tolerate them. Most dogs will enjoy the treat with no adverse health effects. Garlic pills are commonly given to dogs to help ward off bad breath and fleas. If you feed both onions and garlic to a vulnerable dog, the combination could be fatal. Check your vet to be sure that your dog's breed is not affected. Do not feed onions or garlic to the Akita or Shiba breeds.

Common Allergies: Some dogs may be sensitive to dairy products. Usually yogurt, cheese, and powdered milk are tolerated better than whole milk. Other dogs may be allergic to corn, in which case you'd want to omit cornmeal, corn oil, and other corn-based products from a recipe. Individual dogs may not tolerate garlic or onions. Like humans, dogs may have individual food sensitivities.

When in doubt about any food or other substance around the house, garden, or your neighborhood, consult a veterinarian or other dog-nutrition specialist.

Dogs Are Individuals

Remember that each dog has his own needs. You need to tailor your dog's diet to what he can, will, and needs to eat. Here's a cautionary tale.

About 4 years ago I adopted a female Basenji, who I named Apit and who had been neglected and nearly starved to death. It's not that her former owners were deliberately cruel. It's just that they did not know how to feed a dog and paid little attention to the puppy while it was eating.

Apit had a small mouth. What would have been a standard cookie or treat for a small dog was still too large for her. Her previous owners did not seem to notice this, and she was about one-third the normal weight for a dog of her age and size. Every bone in her body seemed visible. The same day I adopted her, I took her to a vet, who examined her and thought she wouldn't make it.

By simply observing her eating habits, I discovered that she would eat tiny pieces of food but turn away large, tasty ones—ones too large for her mouth. Immediately, I began to prepare food more suited to her eating abilities. The results are astounding. Today she's a good fat little girl.

So please, when making dog cookies and treats, make them to your dog's specifications, not yours.

Foods to Avoid

Here are some foods and other items that may be found in your home or garden that must be kept away from your dog and other pets. These foods are toxic to many animals and can even be fatal. Do not hesitate to contact a veterinarian if your dog eats or drinks any of these products.

Alcoholic beverages

Almond kernels

Apple seeds (contain arsenic)

Apricot (kernel in the pit can be fatal)

Avocado leaves, stems, seeds, and outer skin

Bone meal that might be contaminated with scrapie or BSE

> Do not use bone meal purchased in feed-and-grain stores or in questionable outlets.

Caffeine

Castor bean (can be fatal if chewed)

Cherry pits (contain cyanide)

Chocolate or cocoa

Fruit pits (choking)

Garlic (raw or spoiled); garlic powder

> Some dogs do not tolerate garlic or garlic powder.

Meats and meat products that might be contaminated with hoof-and-mouth disease, scrapie (BSE), bacteria, or other viruses

MSG (monosodium glutamate)

Onions (raw or spoiled)

    Do not feed onions to the Akita and Shiba breeds; the effect can be deadly.

Peaches (kernel in the pit, contains cyanide)

Potato leaves and stems

Rhubarb leaves

Tea tree (plant or essential oil)

Tomato leaves and stems

Lip-Smacking Recipes

dobis

This was my first dog treat, created in 1969 while I was living in Roseville, California. Shortly thereafter I moved to Portsmouth, New Hampshire, to establish a factory for manufacturing these treats. I wasn't sure what to call it, and after a moment's thought, called it Dobis. Most people called it "doo-bis," but my intent was to create a word sounding like "dough-bis." *Dobis* combines two words, *dog* and *biscuit,* taking "do-" from *dog* and "bis" from *biscuit.*

This recipe uses desiccated liver, which can be expensive. I've given this recipe to dog owners whose aversion to raw liver was greater than their desire to prepare dog treats.

144 to 168 **cookies**

2 cups whole-wheat flour

$\frac{1}{2}$ cup soy flour

$\frac{1}{2}$ cup nonfat dry milk

$\frac{1}{2}$ cup desiccated bone meal

2 teaspoons brewer's yeast

$\frac{1}{2}$ cup desiccated liver

1 cup vegetable shortening

3 large eggs

$\frac{1}{2}$ to $\frac{3}{4}$ cup fresh beef broth, or sufficient for processing

1. Position the rack in the center of the oven and preheat the oven to 375°F. Have two ungreased cookie sheets or baking trays ready.

2. In a large bowl, use a fork or wire whisk to blend the two flours, dry milk, bone meal, yeast, and liver. Then use a pastry blender or two knives to cut in the shortening until the dough reaches a coarse-crumb stage.

3. In a small bowl, using a wire whisk or electric mixer on MEDIUM speed, beat the eggs and $\frac{1}{2}$ cup beef broth together until smooth.

4. Then use a large spoon, a spatula, or your hand to combine the two mixes, blending until a soft dough forms and pulls away from the sides of the bowl. If the mixture seems dry, add a little more broth, 1 tablespoonful at a time.

5. Turn the dough onto a lightly floured flat surface, and using a rolling pin, roll it out to $1/4$ to $1/2$ inch thick. Use a $1^{1}/_{2}$-inch round cookie cutter to cut out as many cookies as you can, reworking the scraps as you go. The dough will become very stiff as it is reworked.

6. Place the cookies side by side on the baking trays and bake for 18 to 20 minutes or until the cookies appear very dry and the edges are light golden brown. Remove the trays from the oven and cool to room temperature. Turn off the oven.

7. When the oven is just warm, place all the cooled cookies back on one baking tray, and return them to the cooling oven. Leave them undisturbed, without opening the oven door, for 8 to 16 hours.

dobis Variation

I created this simple variation on the Dobis cookies when desiccated liver wasn't readily available or the supply was too expensive.

144 to 168 **cookies**

1 pound raw beef liver

3 large eggs

$1/2$ cup fresh beef broth, or enough for processing

5 cups whole-wheat flour

$1/2$ cup nonfat dry milk

2 tablespoons brewer's yeast

3 tablespoons desiccated bone meal

1. Position the rack in the center of the oven and preheat at 375°F. Have two ungreased baking trays ready.

2. In an electric blender, process the liver on HIGH speed until it becomes a smooth blend. Add the eggs and broth, again processing until very smooth.

3. In a large bowl, using a fork or wire whisk, blend the flour, dry milk, bone meal, yeast, and liver.

4. Using a large spoon, a spatula, or your hand, combine the two mixes, blending until a soft dough forms and pulls away from the sides of the bowl. If the mixture seems dry, add a little more broth 1 tablespoon at a time.

5. Turn the dough onto a lightly floured flat surface, and using a rolling pin, roll out to $1/4$ to $1/2$ inch thick. Use a $1^1/2$ -inch round cookie cutter to cut out as many cookies as you can, reworking the scraps as you go. The dough will become very stiff as it is reworked.

6. Place the cookies side by side on the baking trays and bake for 18 to 20 minutes or until the cookies appear very dry and have a light golden color around the edges. Remove the trays from the oven and cool to room temperature. Turn off the oven.

7. When the oven is just warm, put all the cooled cookies back on one baking tray, and return it to the cooling oven. Leave them undisturbed, without opening the oven door, for 8 to 16 hours.

Nefer's Nuggets

This cookie was named after a mixed-breed Basenji. My dog Nefer was the original inspiration for my dog cookies. He was a sweet, gentle lad, and I cried when he was gone. When I created these treats, he went crazy for them. He loved them so much that I named them in his honor. The word *nuggets* in the recipe title refers to the tiny carob chips.

144 cookies

4 cups whole-wheat flour

$1/4$ cup soy flour

$1/2$ cup nonfat dry milk

3 teaspoons brewer's yeast

$^1/_4$ cup desiccated liver

$1^1/_2$ cups carob chips

1 cup vegetable shortening

3 large eggs

$^1/_2$ cup molasses

$^1/_2$ to $^3/_4$ cup fresh beef broth, or sufficient for processing

1. Position the rack in the center of the oven and preheat at 375°F. Have two ungreased cookie sheets or baking trays ready.

2. In a large bowl, using a fork or wire whisk, blend the whole-wheat flour, soy flour, dry milk, yeast, liver, and carob chips. Then, using a pastry blender or two knives, cut in the shortening until the dough reaches a coarse-crumb stage.

3. In a small bowl, using a wire whisk or electric mixer on MEDIUM speed, beat the egg until foamy before beating in the molasses and $^1/_2$ cup beef broth.

4. Using a large spoon, a spatula, or your hand, combine the two mixes, blending until a soft dough forms and pulls away from the sides of the bowl. If the mixture seems a little dry, add a little more broth, 1 tablespoonful at a time.

5. Turn the dough onto a lightly floured flat surface, and using a rolling pin, roll it out to $^1/_4$ to $^1/_2$ inch thick. Use a $1^1/_2$-inch round cookie cutter to cut out as many cookies as you can, reworking the scraps as you go. The dough will become very stiff.

6. Place the cookies side by side on the baking trays and bake for 18 to 20 minutes or until the cookies appear very dry and the edges are light golden brown. Remove the trays from the oven and cool them to room temperature. Turn off the oven.

7. When they are completely cooled, put all the cookies back on a single baking tray and return them to the cooling oven. Leave them undisturbed, without opening the oven door, for 8 to 16 hours.

Abu's Best

There may be a time when you want to make dog cookies in quantity. Perhaps you want to raise money for your local ASPCA, church, temple, or school. Or you have many dogs at home that you need to feed. If this is the case, then this recipe might work for you. However, you may want to make a small test batch of cookies to make sure the dogs like them.

18 to 20 pounds **cookies**

16 pounds whole-wheat flour

7 ounces nonfat dry milk or whey powder

2 pounds desiccated liver

2 pounds carob chips

8 ounces vegetable shortening

2 pounds eggs (18 whole eggs)

10 ounces molasses

2 tablespoons canola oil

$^1/_2$ cup beef broth, or sufficient for processing

1. Position the rack in the center of the oven and preheat at 375°F. Have two to four ungreased baking trays ready.
2. In a large bowl, using a fork or wire whisk, blend the flour, dry milk, and liver. Using a pastry blender or two knives, cut in the shortening until the dough reaches a coarse-crumb stage.
3. In a small bowl, using a wire whisk or electric mixer on MEDIUM speed, beat the eggs until foamy before beating in the molasses, oil, and $^1/_2$ cup beef broth.
4. Using a large spoon, a spatula, or your hand, combine the two mixes, blending until a soft dough forms and pulls away from the sides of the bowl. If the mixture seems a little dry, add a little more broth, a tablespoonful at a time.

5. Turn the dough onto a lightly floured flat surface, and using a rolling pin, roll it out to $^1/_4$ to $^1/_2$ inch thick. Use a $1^1/_2$-inch round cookie cutter to cut out as many cookies as you can, reworking the scraps as you go. The dough will become very stiff as it is worked.

6. Place the cookies side by side on the baking trays and bake for 18 to 20 minutes or until the cookies appear very dry and the edges are light golden brown. Remove the trays from the oven and cool the cookies to room temperature. Turn off the oven.

7. When the cookies have cooled completely, put all of them on a single baking tray and return them to the cooling oven. Leave them undisturbed, without opening the oven door, for 8 to 16 hours.

Min-Tari's Carrot Cookies

Again, I can do no more than to honor the dogs I have known and loved. In this case, my inspiration was a little female Basenji. If I seem a little partial to Basenjis, it is because they have been the love of my life for more than 35 years. Here we don't use liver in any form. My little girl loved carrots, and to satisfy her need, I created these. These carrot cookies are not for every dog, but those who like carrots will eagerly accept them.

3 to 4 pounds **cookies**

4 cups whole-wheat flour
$^1/_4$ cup soy flour
1 cup wheat bran
$^1/_2$ cup nonfat dry milk
1 cup vegetable shortening
1 cup warmed honey
$1^1/_4$ cups finely shredded carrots
$^1/_4$ cup fresh beef or chicken broth, or sufficient for processing

1. In a large bowl, using a wire whisk, blend the two flours, wheat bran, and dry milk. Then, using two knives or a pastry blender, cut in the shortening until fine crumbs form.

2. In a medium bowl, using a large spoon, combine the honey, carrots, and broth.

3. Using a large spoon, a spatula, or your hand, combine the two mixes, blending until the dry ingredients are just moistened and a stiff dough is formed. Place the dough in a plastic bag, seal it tight, and leave it in the refrigerator for about 8 hours.

4. When you're ready to make the cookies, position the rack in the center of the oven and pre-heat at 375°F. Have two ungreased baking trays ready.

5. Turn the dough onto a lightly floured flat surface, and using a rolling pin, roll it out to $1/4$ to $1/2$ inch thick. Use a $1 1/2$-inch round cookie cutter to cut out as many cookies as you can, reworking the scraps as you go. The dough will become very stiff as it is reworked.

6. Place the cookies side by side on the baking trays and bake for about 18 to 20 minutes or until the cookies appear very dry and the edges are light golden brown. Remove the trays from the oven and cool to room temperature. Turn off the oven.

7. When the cookies have cooled completely, put all of them on a single baking tray and return them to the cooling oven. Leave them undisturbed, without opening the oven door, for 8 to 16 hours.

Tegga's Terrific Treats

Tegga is the newest member of my family, and unfortunately he has lived up to his nick-name, "The Kid from Hell." Only people who have lived through and experienced the puppyhood of a Basenji can understand the meaning of these words. Well, this pup will eat anything in the house, hence his name. One of Tegga's particular favorites is peanut butter.

3 to 4 pounds **cookies**

3 cups whole-wheat flour

1 cup unbleached all-purpose flour

$1/4$ cup soy flour or white corn flour

$1/4$ cup desiccated liver

Yum

$^3/_4$ cup wheat bran

$^1/_2$ cup nonfat dry milk

2 teaspoon brewer's yeast

2 large eggs

1 cup creamy-style peanut butter

1 cup fresh beef broth, or sufficient for processing

1. Position the rack in the center of the oven and preheat at 375°F. Have two ungreased baking trays ready.
2. In a large bowl, using a fork or wire whisk, blend the three flours, liver, wheat bran, dry milk, and yeast.
3. In a medium bowl, using a wire whisk or electric mixer on MEDIUM speed, beat together the eggs, peanut butter, and beef broth until smooth.
4. Using a large spoon, a spatula, or your hand, combine the two mixes, blending until the dry ingredients form into a soft dough and pull away from the sides of the bowl.
5. Turn the dough onto a lightly floured flat surface, and using a rolling pin, roll it out to $^1/_4$ to $^1/_2$ inch thick. Use a $1^1/_2$-inch round cookie cutter to cut out as many cookies as you can, reworking the scraps as you go. The dough will become very stiff as it is reworked.
6. Place the cookies side by side on the baking trays and bake for about 18 to 20 minutes or until the cookies appear very dry and the edges turn light golden brown. Remove the trays from the oven and cool to room temperature. Turn off the oven.
7. When the cookies have cooled completely, put all of them on a single baking tray and return them to the cooling oven. Leave them undisturbed, without opening the oven door, for 8 to 16 hours.

   PLEASE NOTE: Some dogs may be allergic to corn-based products.

Animal-Shelter Puppy Treats

Years ago a woman at a local animal shelter gave me this recipe. She explained that large commercial cookies and treats were too big for puppies and small dogs at the shelter. Someone working at the shelter occasionally made these to fit into the little mouths of small dogs.

24 small **balls**

2/3 cup wheat germ

1/4 cup nonfat dry milk

two 4-ounce jars beef-flavored or chicken-flavored baby food

1. Position the rack in the center of the oven and preheat at 350°F. Have an ungreased baking tray ready.

2. In a medium bowl, using a large fork, blend the wheat germ and the dry milk, and work in the baby food to make a soft dough. Pinch off small pieces about the size of small green olives, and roll them between floured hands to form small balls.

3. Place each ball about $1/2$ inch apart on the prepared baking sheet, and flatten with the back of a fork. Bake for about 25 to 30 minutes or until the cookies feel hard to the touch.

4. Remove from the oven and cool on a wire rack. Allow to air-dry for at least 3 hours before placing them in a container with a loose-fitting cover.

PLEASE NOTE: Some dogs may be sensitive to dairy products.

Apit's Love Cookies

Apit is the most recent addition to our house; she came to me after Tegga. Unlike Tegga, she was a stray who hadn't been abused, but she certainly hadn't been fed. There wasn't a bone in her little body that didn't show. An average pencil would be of greater diameter than her legs. Well, she's fatter now, and these were one of the foods that helped. These cookies are Apit's favorites.

1 to 2 pounds **cookies**

2 cups whole-wheat flour

1 cup yellow cornmeal

2 tablespoons brewer's yeast

2 tablespoons desiccated bone meal

2 teaspoons garlic powder

2 large eggs

1 to $^1/_2$ cups fresh beef or chicken broth, or sufficient for processing

1. Position the rack in the center of the oven and preheat at 375°F. Have two ungreased baking trays ready.

2. In a large bowl, using a fork or wire whisk, blend the flour, cornmeal, yeast, bone meal, and garlic powder.

3. In a small bowl, using a wire whisk or electric mixer on MEDIUM speed, beat the eggs until they're foamy before beating in 1 cup beef broth.

4. Using a large spoon, a spatula, or your hands, combine the two mixes, blending until the mixture forms into a soft dough and pulls away from the sides of the bowl.

5. Turn the dough onto a lightly floured flat surface, and using a rolling pin, roll it out to $^1/_4$ to $^1/_2$ inch thick. Use a $1^1/_2$ -inch round cookie cutter to cut out as many cookies as you can, reworking the scraps as you go. The dough will become very stiff as it is reworked.

6. Place the cookies side by side on the baking trays. Bake for 18 to 20 minutes or until the cookies appear very dry and the edges are light golden brown. Remove the trays from the oven and cool to room temperature. Turn off the oven.

7. When the cookies have cooled completely, put all of them on a single baking tray and return them to the cooling oven. Leave them undisturbed, without opening the oven door, for 8 to 16 hours.

PLEASE NOTE: Some dogs may be allergic to corn-based products or garlic.

HoneY-Love BiScUits

Every dog expert will tell you that sugar isn't something you feed to dogs. Well, I have been feeding dogs cookies that contain honey for the past 30 to 35 years, and they've never had any ill effects. Of course, honey is more healthful than sugar.

2 to 3 pounds **cookies**

2½ cups whole-wheat flour

½ cup soy flour or white corn flour

½ cups nonfat dry milk

6 tablespoons vegetable shortening

1 large egg

½ cup honey

½ cup fresh beef or chicken broth, or sufficient for processing

1. Position the rack in the center of the oven and preheat at 350°F. Have two ungreased baking trays ready.

2. In a large bowl, using a fork or wire whisk, combine the two flours and dry milk. Using a pastry cutter or two knives, cut in the shortening until the mixture resembles fine crumbs.

3. In a small bowl, using a wire whisk or electric mixer on MEDIUM speed, beat the egg until foamy before beating in the honey and broth.

4. Using a large spoon, a spatula, or your hands, combine the two mixes, blending until the mixture pulls away from the sides of the bowl and forms a soft dough.

5. Turn the dough onto a lightly floured flat surface, and using a rolling pin, roll it out to $1/4$ to $1/2$ inch thick. Use a $1^1/2$ -inch round cookie cutter to cut out as many cookies as you can, reworking the scraps as you go. The dough will become very stiff as it is reworked.

6. Place the cookies side by side on the baking trays and bake for 18 to 20 minutes or until the cookies appear very dry and the edges are light golden brown. Remove the trays from the oven and cool to room temperature. Turn off the oven.

7. When the cookies have cooled completely, put all of them on a single baking tray and return them to the cooling oven. Leave them undisturbed, without opening the oven door, for 8 to 16 hours.

PLEASE NOTE: Some dogs may be allergic to corn-based products. These cookies also contain honey.

Manu's Favorite Lamb Treats

For dogs, lamb is one of the most digestible of all meats. Vets are sure to tell you that a diet that includes lamb and rice is great for your dog.

2 to 3 pounds cookies

2 cups whole-wheat flour

$^1/_2$ cup rice flour

1 cup cooked and finely minced ground lamb

$^1/_2$ cup nonfat dry milk

1 large egg

$^1/_3$ cup canola oil

$^3/_4$ cup plus 1 tablespoon fresh lamb broth, beef broth, or drippings

1. Position the rack in the center of the oven and preheat at 350°F. Have two ungreased baking trays ready.
2. In a large bowl, using a fork or wire whisk, blend the whole-wheat flour, rice flour, dry milk, and cooked lamb.
3. In a medium bowl, using a wire whisk or electric mixer on MEDIUM speed, beat the egg until foamy before beating in the oil and broth.
4. Using a large spoon, a spatula, or your hands, blend the two mixes until a soft dough forms and the dough pulls away from the sides of the bowl.
5. Turn the dough onto a lightly floured flat surface, and using a rolling pin, roll out to $^1/_4$ inch thick. Use a $1^1/_2$-inch round cookie cutter to cut out as many cookies as you can, reworking the scraps as you go. The dough will become very stiff as it is reworked.
6. Place the cookies side by side on the baking trays and bake for about 18 to 20 minutes or until the cookies appear very dry and the edges are light golden brown. Remove the trays from the oven and cool to room temperature. Turn off the oven.

7. When the cookies have cooled completely, put all of them on a single baking tray and return them to the cooling oven. Leave them undisturbed, without opening the oven door, for 8 to 16 hours.

PLEASE NOTE: Some dogs may be sensitive to dairy products.

Lamb Cookies

Although lamb drippings are asked for in these cookies, if they aren't available, you can use any meat drippings. The most important thing in making these cookies is to be sure the drippings are fresh.

1 to 2 pounds **cookies**

2 cups whole-wheat flour

1 cup rice flour

$1/2$ cup nonfat dry milk

$1/3$ cup vegetable shortening

2 large eggs

$3/4$ cup fresh lamb drippings, or sufficient for processing

1. Position the rack in the center of the oven and preheat at 350ºF. Lightly grease or use parchment paper to line two cookie sheets or baking trays.

2. In a large bowl, using a fork or wire whisk, blend the whole-wheat flour, rice flour, and dry milk. Using a pastry blender or two knives, cut in the shortening until the mixture resembles a coarse meal.

3. In a small bowl, using a wire whisk or electric mixer on MEDIUM speed, beat the eggs until foamy before beating in the drippings.

4. Using a large spoon, a spatula, or your hands, combine the two mixes until a soft dough forms and pulls away from the sides of the bowl.

5. Turn the dough onto a lightly floured flat surface, and using a rolling pin, roll out to $1/4$ inch thick. Use a $1^1/2$ -inch round cookie cutter to cut out as many cookies as you can, reworking the scraps as you go. The dough will become stiff as it is reworked.

6. Place the cookies side by side on the prepared baking trays and bake for 18 to 20 minutes or until the cookies appear very dry and the edges are light golden brown. Remove the trays from the oven and cool to room temperature. Turn off the oven.

7. When the cookies have cooled completely, put all of them on a single baking tray and return them to the cooling oven. Leave them undisturbed, without opening the oven door, for 8 to 16 hours.

PLEASE NOTE: Some dogs may be sensitive to dairy products.

Meat & garlic Cookies

Vets have recommended that I use garlic pills to correct a dog's bad breath. It does work! At the same time, instead of fighting a dog to push a pill down its throat, why not include the garlic in a treat the dog will readily eat?

1 to 2 pounds **cookies**

$2^1/2$ **cups whole-wheat flour**

$1/2$ **cup rice flour**

$1/2$ **cup nonfat dry milk**

$1/2$ **teaspoon garlic powder**

1 cup cooked ground meat, finely minced

2 large eggs

1 cup beef or chicken drippings, or sufficient for processing

1. Position the rack in the center of the oven and preheat at 350°F. Lightly grease or line with parchment two cookie sheets.

2. In a large bowl, using a fork or wire whisk, blend the whole-wheat flour, rice flour, dry milk, garlic powder, and meat. Be sure the meat is well coated and separated.

3. In a small bowl, using a wire whisk or electric mixer on MEDIUM speed, beat the eggs and drippings together.

4. Using a large spoon, a spatula, or your hands, combine the two mixes, blending until the mixture pulls away from the sides of the bowl and forms a soft dough.

5. Turn the dough onto a lightly floured flat surface, and using a rolling pin, roll out to $1/4$ inch thick. Use a $1^1/2$-inch round cookie cutter to cut out as many cookies as you can, reworking the scraps as you go. The dough will become stiff as it is reworked.

6. Place the cookies side by side on the prepared cookie sheets or baking trays. Bake for 18 to 20 minutes or until the cookies appear very dry and the edges are light golden brown. Remove the trays from the oven and cool to room temperature. Turn off the oven.

7. When the cookies have cooled completely, put all of them on a single baking tray and return them to the cooling oven. Leave them undisturbed, without opening the oven door, for 8 to 16 hours.

PLEASE NOTE: Some dogs may be allergic to garlic.

doggie BaLLs

Remember the old expression parents use when speaking to a child: "Don't play with your food." However, we encourage dogs to play with these doggie balls. Dogs will be more than eager to eat the food they first play with.

3 to 4 pounds **cookies**

1 tablespoon active dry yeast

$^1/_4$ cup warm water

$^1/_3$ cup honey

$4^1/_4$ cups all-purpose flour

2 cups whole-wheat flour

$^3/_4$ cup soy flour or white corn flour

$^1/_2$ cup graham flour

$^1/_2$ cup nonfat dry milk

4 teaspoons kelp powder

$3^3/_4$ cups beef or chicken broth, or sufficient for processing

1. In a small bowl, combine the yeast, water, and honey. Wait 10 minutes.
2. Position the rack in the center of the oven and preheat at 350ºF. Lightly grease or use parchment paper to line two cookie sheets or baking trays.
3. In a large bowl, using a fork or wire whisk, blend the four flours, dry milk, and kelp powder. Make an indentation in the center of the mixture and pour in the yeast mixture and 3 cups of broth. Using a large spoon or spatula, blend until the mixture pulls away from the sides of the bowl and a smooth dough forms. If the mixture seems a little dry, add more broth $^1/_4$ cup at a time.
4. Pinch off small pieces of dough and roll them between floured hands to shape them into small balls about the size of large walnuts.
5. Place the balls on the prepared baking sheets and bake for about 18 to 20 minutes or until the balls are a rich golden color. Remove from the oven and cool on a wire rack. They

may be dried as directed in the previous recipes, and/or stored in a loosely covered container and served as desired.

garLic NUgget BaLLs

Garlic nuggets are the tiny pieces of garlic included in the ingredients. The secret of making these is to be sure the garlic cloves are as finely minced as possible. These balls also make great toys your dog can play with before eating them.

36 to 48 **balls**

3 cups whole-wheat flour

$1/4$ cup rice flour

1 cup yellow cornmeal

1 cup oat bran

$1/2$ cup nonfat dry milk

$1/4$ cup vegetable shortening

2 cloves garlic, chopped very fine

3 large eggs

1 cup slightly warm beef or chicken drippings, or sufficient for processing

1. Position the rack in the center of the oven and preheat at 350°F. Lightly grease or line with parchment paper two cookie sheets or baking trays.
2. In a large bowl, using a fork or wire whisk, blend the flour, cornmeal, oat bran, and dry milk. Using a pastry blender or two knives, cut in the shortening until the mixture resembles fine crumbs. Stir in the garlic.
3. In a medium bowl, using a wire whisk or electric mixer, beat the eggs until foamy. Continue beating and add the drippings.

4. Using a large spoon, a spatula, or your hands, combine the two mixes, blending until the mixture pulls away from the sides of the bowl and forms a soft dough. Pinch off small pieces of dough and roll them between floured hands to form small balls about the size of walnuts.

5. Place the balls on the prepared baking sheets and bake for about 18 to 20 minutes or until the balls are a rich golden brown. Remove from the oven and cool on a wire rack. They may be oven-dried or stored in a non-airtight container and served as desired.

PLEASE NOTE: Some dogs may be allergic to corn-based products or garlic.

Corn-doggie dogs

While walking through a state fair, the idea came to me: "People love corn dogs. Why not have the same thing for dogs?" So I set out to create them. These corn-doggie treats were the result.

36 to 48 **corn dogs**

1 cup whole-wheat flour

1 cup yellow cornmeal

2 teaspoons baking powder

1 large egg

1 cup milk, or sufficient for processing

$\frac{1}{2}$ cup bacon drippings

four 5-inch frankfurters or hot dogs, each cut into 10 slices

1. Position the rack in the center of the oven and preheat at 350°F. Lightly grease the bottoms of a 12-cup, $1\frac{1}{4}$-inch (small-size) muffin pan.

2. In a large bowl, using a fork or wire whisk, blend the flour, cornmeal, and baking powder.

3. In a medium bowl, using a wire whisk or electric mixer, beat the egg until foamy and doubled in volume. Beat in the milk and bacon drippings.

4. Using a large spoon or spatula, combine the two mixes, blending until the dry ingredients are just moistened.

5. Drop 1 teaspoonful of the mixture into each cup of the prepared muffin pan and press a slice of frankfurter into the center of each, topping it with an additional $1/2$ teaspoon of the mixture.

6. Bake for about 15 to 20 minutes or until the tops are a golden brown color and a wooden toothpick inserted into the cups comes out clean. Remove the pan from the oven and cool it on a wire rack before removing the dogs to a wire rack to cool completely. Store these corn-doggies in the refrigerator.

PLEASE NOTE: Some dogs may be allergic to corn-based products.

Carrot & Cheese dog Treats

To a dog's taste buds, a carrot is sweet. When you add cheese to the carrot taste, your dog will quickly gobble down these treats. After they have dried, you can easily store these cookies or take them on a trip or vacation. Warning: your dog will love them; so keep plenty on hand.

160 **cookies**

$1^1/_2$ cups whole-wheat flour

$1^1/_2$ cups unbleached all-purpose flour

2 tablespoon grated dried cheese

$1/_2$ pound lean ground beef, cooked and finely minced

1 large carrot, trimmed, pared, and finely grated

$1/_2$ teaspoon garlic powder

2 large eggs

$1/_2$ cup beef or chicken broth or drippings, or sufficient for processing

1. Position the rack in the center of the oven and preheat at 350°F. Lightly grease or use parchment paper to line two cookie sheets or baking trays.
2. In a large bowl combine the whole-wheat flour, unbleached all-purpose flour, cheese, cooked beef, carrots, and garlic powder.
3. In a small bowl, using a wire whisk or electric mixer on MEDIUM speed, beat the eggs until foamy before beating in the broth.
4. Using a large spoon, a spatula, or your hands, combine the two mixes, blending until the mixture pulls away from the sides of the bowl and forms a soft dough. If the mixture seems a little dry, add a little more broth, a tablespoonful at a time.
5. Turn the dough onto a lightly floured flat surface, and using a rolling pin, roll out to $1/_4$ inch thick. Use a $1^1/_2$-inch round cookie cutter to cut out as many cookies as you can, reworking the scraps as you go. The dough will become stiff as it is reworked.
6. Place the cookies side by side on the prepared cookie sheets and bake for 20 to 23

minutes or until the cookies appear very dry and the edges are light golden brown. Remove the trays from the oven and cool to room temperature. Turn off the oven.

7. When the cookies have cooled completely, put all of them on a single cookie sheet and return them to the cooling oven. Leave them undisturbed, without opening the oven door, for 8 to 16 hours.

   PLEASE NOTE: Some dogs may be allergic to garlic or garlic powder.

Quickie Turkey dog Treats

If you don't have time to make the more complicated recipes in this collection, at least try these quickie treats. They're so easy to prepare and dogs love them so much! Give your pet a chance to taste something that's a whistle to make and that's really yummy.

30 **cookies**

$1^3/_4$ **cups whole-wheat flour**

two 4.5-ounce jars turkey-flavored baby food

$^1/_2$ **cup beef broth, or sufficient for processing**

1. Position the rack in the center of the oven and preheat at 350°F. Lightly grease or use parchment paper to line a cookie sheet or baking tray.

2. In a large bowl, using a fork, combine the flour and baby food, mixing until they are well blended and form into a very soft dough. If the mixture is a little dry, add beef broth, $^1/_4$ cup at a time, until the mixture pulls away from the sides of the bowl.

3. Pinch off small pieces of the dough, and between floured hands, roll them into small balls. Place the balls on the prepared baking sheet $^1/_2$ inch apart and flatten them with the back of the fork to $^1/_4$ inch thick.

4. Bake for about 18 to 20 minutes or until the tops are golden brown. Remove the pan from the oven and allow the cookies to cool to room temperature on a wire rack. They may be dried as directed in the previous recipes, or stored in a non-airtight container and served as desired.

Liver Treats

These are a great treat for dogs. But be warned, you'll be tempted to feed your dog more of these than you really should. Yes, your dog will love them!

125 cookies

$3^1/_4$ **cups whole-wheat flour**

$1^1/_2$ **cups white corn flour**

$^1/_2$ **teaspoon garlic powder**

1 pound raw beef liver

1 large egg

2 tablespoons canola oil or corn oil

3 tablespoons fresh beef or chicken drippings or broth, or sufficient for processing

1. Position the rack in the center of the oven and preheat at 350°F. Lightly grease or use parchment paper to line two cookie sheets or baking trays.
2. In a large bowl, using a fork or wire whisk, blend the whole-wheat flour, white corn flour, and garlic powder.
3. In a blender, process the liver on HIGH until it becomes a smooth paste. Add the egg, oil, and drippings, and process until smooth.
4. Using a large spoon, a spatula, or your hands, combine the two mixes, blending until the mixture pulls away from the sides of the bowl and forms a soft dough. If the mixture seems a little dry, add a little more broth, a tablespoonful at a time.
5. Turn the dough onto a lightly floured flat surface, and using a rolling pin, roll out to $^1/_4$ inch thick. Use a $1^1/_2$-inch round cookie cutter to cut out as many cookies as you can, reworking the scraps as you go. The dough will become stiff as it is reworked.
6. Place the cookies side by side on the prepared cookie sheets or baking trays. Bake for 20 to 25 minutes or until the cookies appear very dry and the edges are light golden brown. Remove the trays from the oven and cool to room temperature. Turn off the oven.

7. When the cookies have cooled completely, put all of them on a single baking tray or cookie sheet and return them to the cooling oven. Leave them undisturbed, without opening the oven door, for 8 to 16 hours.

PLEASE NOTE: Some dogs may be allergic to corn-based products or garlic.

Tuna Treats

We must never forget the varied diets of dogs in all parts of the world. Although their main
food is usually considered to be meat, there are those who have a very healthful diet of
fish. Dogs are very fond of this simple little treat.

140 **cookies**

2 cups whole-wheat flour

$1/2$ cup soy flour

$1/2$ cup yellow cornmeal

$1/4$ cup canola oil or corn oil

1 cup milk, or sufficient for processing

6-ounce can chunk tuna in water, drained

1. Position the rack in the center of the oven and preheat at 350°F. Lightly grease or use
parchment paper to line two cookie sheets or baking trays.

2. In a large bowl, using a fork or wire whisk, blend the whole-wheat flour, soy flour, and
cornmeal.

3. In a small bowl, using a fork, combine the oil, milk, and tuna, stirring until well blended.
Make an indentation in the center of the flour mixture and pour in the tuna mixture.
Using a large spoon or spatula, blend until this mixture pulls away from the sides of the
bowl and a smooth dough forms. If it seems a little dry, add more milk $1/4$ cup at a time.

4. Turn the dough onto a lightly floured flat surface and using a rolling pin, roll out to $1/4$ inch thick. Use a $1^1/_2$-inch round cookie cutter to cut out as many cookies as you can, reworking the scraps as you go. The dough will become stiff as it is reworked.

5. Place the cookies side by side on the prepared cookie sheets and bake for 20 to 23 minutes or until the cookies appear very dry and the edges are light golden brown. Remove the trays from the oven and cool to room temperature. Turn off the oven.

6. When the cookies have cooled completely, put all of them on a single baking tray and return them to the cooling oven. Leave them undisturbed, without opening the oven door, for 8 to 16 hours. Note: These cookies keep very well without going bad after they have been dried as directed above. Also, remember these cookies contain cornmeal.

PLEASE NOTE: Some dogs may be allergic to corn-based products.

Coming-through-the-Rye Treats

Rye is another one of those flavors that tastes distinctly different when smelled or eaten by a dog and by a human being. To dogs, rye flour is sweet, and it imparts much of its flavor to everything blended with it. The oats in these cookies will absorb the flavor from the liver.

175 to 200 cookies

$1^1/_2$ cups whole-wheat flour

$1^1/_2$ cups unbleached all-purpose flour

1 cup rye flour

1 cup rolled oats

1 cup yellow cornmeal

$^1/_4$ cup desiccated liver

$^1/_2$ teaspoon garlic powder

2 large eggs

$^1/_2$ cup canola oil or corn oil

$1^3/_4$ to 2 cups beef or chicken broth

1. Position the rack in the center of the oven and preheat at 350ºF. Lightly grease or use parchment paper to line two cookie sheets or baking trays.

2. In a large bowl, using a fork or wire whisk, blend the three flours, oats, cornmeal, liver powder, and garlic powder.

3. In a medium bowl, using a wire whisk or electric mixer on MEDIUM speed, beat the eggs, oil, and broth together until smooth.

4. Using a large spoon, a spatula, or your hands, combine the two mixes, blending until the mixture pulls away from the sides of the bowl and forms a soft dough. If the mixture seems a little dry, add a little more broth, a tablespoonful at a time.

5. Turn the dough onto a lightly floured flat surface, and using a rolling pin, roll out to $^1/_4$ inch thick. Use a $1^1/_2$-inch round cookie cutter to cut out as many cookies as you can, reworking the scraps as you go. The dough will become stiff as it is reworked.

6. Place the cookies side by side on the prepared cookie sheets or baking trays. Bake for 20 to 25 minutes or until the cookies appear very dry and the edges are light golden brown. Remove the trays from the oven and cool to room temperature. Turn off the oven.

7. When the cookies have cooled completely, put all of them on a single baking tray and return them to the cooling oven. Leave them undisturbed, without opening the oven door, for 8 to 16 hours.

   PLEASE NOTE: Some dogs may be allergic to garlic or corn.

Flea-Away Biscuits

I don't know who created these original cookies or how someone got the notion that garlic wards off fleas. However, I do know that when garlic—raw, cooked, or powdered—is used in greater quantity than other foods or ingredients, it will do little more than give a dog bad breath. Do not exceed the amount of garlic powder given.

125 cookies

1 cup whole-wheat flour

1 cup unbleached all-purpose flour

$\frac{1}{2}$ cup whole-wheat bran

$\frac{1}{2}$ cup brewer's yeast

2 tablespoons garlic powder

3 tablespoons canola oil or corn oil

1 cup plus 2 tablespoons beef or chicken drippings or broth

1. Position the rack in the center of the oven and preheat at 350°F. Lightly grease or use parchment paper to line two cookie sheets or baking trays.
2. In a large bowl, using a fork or wire whisk, blend the two flours, bran, yeast, and garlic powder. Make an indentation in the center of the mixture and pour in the oil and drippings, and using a large spoon or a spatula, blend until the mixture pulls away from the sides of the bowl and a smooth dough forms.
3. Using a large spoon, a spatula, or your hands, combine the two mixes, blending until the mixture pulls away from the sides of the bowl and forms a soft dough. If the mixture seems a little dry, add a little more broth, a tablespoonful at a time.
4. Turn the dough onto a lightly floured flat surface, and using a rolling pin, roll out to $\frac{1}{4}$ inch thick. Use a $1\frac{1}{2}$-inch round cookie cutter to cut out as many cookies as you can, reworking the scraps as you go. The dough will become stiff as it is reworked.
5. Place the cookies side by side on the prepared cookie sheets or baking trays and bake for 20 to 25 minutes or until the cookies appear very dry and the edges are light golden

brown. Remove the trays from the oven and cool to room temperature. Turn off the oven.

6. When the cookies have cooled completely, put all of them on a single baking tray and return them to the cooling oven. Leave them undisturbed, without opening the oven door, for 8 to 16 hours.

PLEASE NOTE: Some dogs may be allergic to garlic or corn-based products.

Beef Your Baby Treats

Any baby food, when used in a treat or as part of a regular diet, is usually considered good for dogs. These treats incorporate the benefits of beef baby food, and dogs love them.

115 to 125 **cookies**

2 cups whole-wheat flour

$1/4$ cup rice flour

$1/2$ cup nonfat dry milk

$1/2$ cup brewer's yeast

2 tablespoons desiccated bone meal

2 large eggs

1 cup canola oil or corn oil

4.5-ounce jar beef baby food

$1/2$ cup beef drippings, or sufficient for processing

1. Position the rack in the center of the oven and preheat at 350°F. Lightly grease or use parchment paper to line two cookie sheets or baking trays.
2. In a large bowl, using a fork or wire whisk, blend the two flours, dry milk powder, yeast, and bone meal.
3. In a medium bowl, using a wire whisk or electric mixer on MEDIUM speed, beat the eggs until foamy, before beating in the oil, baby food, and drippings.

4. Using a large spoon, a spatula, or your hands, combine the two mixes, blending until the mixture pulls away from the sides of the bowl and forms a soft dough. If the mixture seems a little dry, add a little more of the drippings, a tablespoonful at a time.

5. Turn the dough onto a lightly floured flat surface, and using a rolling pin, roll out to $1/4$ inch thick. Use a $1^1/2$-inch round cookie cutter to cut out as many cookies as you can, reworking the scraps as you go. The dough will become stiff as it is reworked.

6. Place the cookies side by side on the prepared cookie sheets or baking trays and bake for 20 to 25 minutes or until the cookies appear very dry and the edges are light golden brown. Remove the trays from the oven and cool to room temperature. Turn off the oven.

7. When the cookies have cooled completely, put all of them on a single baking tray and return them to the cooling oven. Leave them undisturbed, without opening the oven door, for 8 to 16 hours.

Liver & Cheese Cookies

The name of these cookies almost sounds good enough to serve for dinner at your own table. Yes, you can snack on these liver and cheese cookies, too. Like all the cookies in this cookbook, they're fit for human consumption. They won't all suit your palate, however.

100 cookies

2 cups whole-wheat flour

$1/2$ cup soy flour

$1/2$ cup desiccated bone meal

$1^3/4$ cups finely grated cheddar cheese

1 pound raw beef liver

2 tablespoons of beef or chicken broth, or sufficient for processing

1. Position the rack in the center of the oven and preheat at 350°F. Lightly grease or use parchment paper to line two cookie sheets or baking trays.

2. In a large bowl, using a fork or wire whisk, blend the two flours, bone meal, and cheese.

3. In a blender, process the liver until smooth. Beat in the broth.

4. Using a large spoon, a spatula, or your hands, combine the two mixes, blending until the mixture pulls away from the sides of the bowl and forms a soft dough. If the mixture seems dry, add a little more broth 1 tablespoon at a time; if a little wet, add whole-wheat flour 2 tablespoons at a time.

5. Turn the dough onto a lightly floured flat surface, and using a rolling pin, roll out the dough to $1/4$ inch thick. Use a $1^1/2$-inch round cookie cutter to cut out as many cookies as you can, reworking the scraps as you go. The dough will become stiff as it is reworked.

6. Place the cookies side by side on the prepared cookie sheets or baking trays. Bake for 20 to 25 minutes or until the cookies appear very dry and the edges are light golden brown. Remove the trays from the oven and cool to room temperature. Turn off the oven.

7. When the cookies have cooled completely, put all of them on a single baking tray and return them to the cooling oven. Leave them undisturbed, without opening the oven door, for 8 to 16 hours.

Green & gold doggie cookies

While these cookies do not meet the full nutritional requirements for a complete daily diet for a dog, they do come very close. Although they are nearly complete, do not use them to replace a complete, balanced meal.

30 to 36 cookies

1½ cups whole-wheat flour

1 tablespoon grated dried cheese

¼ teaspoon garlic powder

¼ cup vegetable shortening

1 cup cooked frozen peas and corn mix

4 ounces raw liver

1 large egg

¼ cup beef broth, or sufficient for processing

1. Position the rack in the center of the oven and preheat at 350°F. Lightly grease or use parchment paper to line a cookie sheet or baking tray.
2. In a large bowl, using a fork or wire whisk, blend the flour, cheese, and garlic powder. Then, using a pastry blender or two knives, cut in the shortening until the mixture resembles fine crumbs. Stir in the peas and corn.
3. In a blender, process the liver until smooth. Beat in the egg until well blended.
4. Using a large spoon, a spatula, or your hands, combine the two mixes, blending until the mixture pulls away from the sides of the bowl and forms a soft dough. If the mixture seems a little dry, add a little broth, a tablespoonful at a time.
5. Turn the dough onto a lightly floured flat surface, and using a rolling pin, roll it out to ¼ inch thick. Use a 1½-inch round cookie cutter to cut out as many cookies as you can, reworking the scraps as you go. The dough will become stiff as it is reworked.
6. Place the cookies side by side on the prepared baking trays and bake for 20 to 25 minutes

or until the cookies appear very dry and the edges are light golden brown. Remove the trays from the oven and cool to room temperature. Turn off the oven.

7. When the cookies have cooled completely, put all of them on a single baking tray and return them to the cooling oven. Leave them undisturbed, without opening the oven door, for 8 to 16 hours.

PLEASE NOTE: Some dogs may be allergic to garlic or corn.

Lazy Man's dog Cookies

All the work and planning are easily taken out of your hands with these cookies. There's nothing to do but to add the love you feel for the little four-legged friend at your feet.

1 pound **cookies**

4 ounces raw beef liver or pork liver

8.5-ounce box corn-muffin mix

$^1/_2$ teaspoon garlic powder

1. Position the rack in the center of the oven and preheat at 350°F. Lightly grease a $10^1/_2$ x 7 x $1^1/_2$-inch baking pan.

2. In a blender, process the liver until smooth.

3. In a medium bowl, using a large spoon or fork, blend the corn-muffin mix and garlic powder. Pour in the liver from the blender and mix until well incorporated.

4. Spread evenly into the prepared baking pan and bake for 10 to 15 minutes or until the top is a dry golden brown color. Remove from the oven, and using a small spatula, score the top of the cookies into small bite-size squares and cool on a wire rack for 10 minutes before cutting the scored lines through and removing the cookies.

5. Let the cookies air-dry for 8 to 10 hours before storing in a container with a loose-fitting cover.

PLEASE NOTE: Some dogs may be allergic to corn-based products or garlic.

doggie Oatmeal Cookies

These are great cookies, especially if you want to take them with you when you and your dog leave home for a day or two. They keep well if dried even under stressful conditions like camping trips or dog shows. Dogs will love them.

$1^1/2$ pounds **cookies**

$2^1/3$ cups whole-wheat flour

$2/3$ cup rice flour

1 cup uncooked rolled oats

$2/3$ pounds raw beef, pork, or lamb liver

2 tablespoons beef or chicken broth, or sufficient for processing

2 large eggs

1. Position the rack in the center of the oven and preheat at 350°F. Lightly grease or use parchment paper to line two cookie sheets or baking trays.
2. In a large bowl, using a fork or wire whisk, blend the whole-wheat flour, rice flour, and oats.
3. In a blender, process the liver until smooth. Beat in the broth and eggs until well blended.
4. Using a large spoon, a spatula, or your hands, combine the two mixes, blending until the mixture pulls away from the sides of the bowl and forms a soft dough. If the mixture seems a little dry, add a little broth, a tablespoonful at a time.
5. Turn the dough onto a lightly floured flat surface, and using a rolling pin, roll it out to $1/4$ inch thick. Use a $1^1/2$-inch round cookie cutter to cut out as many cookies as you can, reworking the scraps as you go. The dough will become stiff as it is reworked.
6. Place the cookies side by side on the prepared baking trays and bake for 20 to 25 minutes or until the cookies appear very dry and the edges are light golden brown. Remove the trays from the oven and cool to room temperature. Turn off the oven.
7. When the cookies have cooled completely, put all of them on a single baking tray and return them to the cooling oven. Leave them undisturbed, without opening the oven door, for 8 to 16 hours.

NOTE: If rice flour isn't available, then all whole-wheat flour can be used, but it's best to use rice flour if possible.

Healthy Liver Treats

For years, people have been using a product called textured vegetable protein (TVP), which is processed soybeans. This product enhances the protein value of any food cooked with it. Another advantage of using TVP is that it assumes the flavor of the most dominant flavor found in the mixture. In this recipe, TVP will take on the taste and flavor of the liver.

1¼ pounds (90 **cookies** per pound)

1 pound raw beef or pork liver

¼ cup warm water

1 cup textured vegetable protein (TVP)

1½ cups whole-wheat flour

½ cup wheat germ

½ cup oat bran

¼ teaspoon garlic powder

milk (optional), as needed

1. In a blender, process the liver on HIGH until smooth. Beat in the water.
2. In a medium bowl, using a fork, blend the liver and vegetable protein and set aside for 5 minutes.
3. Meanwhile, in a large bowl, using a fork or wire whisk, blend the flour, wheat germ, oat bran, and garlic powder.
4. Using a large spoon, a spatula, or your hands, combine the two mixes, blending until the mixture pulls away from the sides of the bowl and forms a soft dough. If the mixture seems a little dry, add a little milk, a tablespoonful at a time.

5. Turn the dough onto a lightly floured flat surface, and using a rolling pin, roll out to $\frac{1}{4}$ inch thick. Use a $1\frac{1}{2}$-inch round cookie cutter to cut out as many cookies as you can, reworking the scraps as you go. The dough will become stiff as it is reworked.

6. Place the cookies side by side on prepared lightly greased or parchment-paper lined cookie sheets or baking trays. Bake for 20 to 25 minutes or until the cookies appear very dry and the edges are light golden brown. Remove the trays from the oven and cool to room temperature. Turn off the oven.

7. When the cookies have cooled completely, put all of them on a single baking tray and return them to the cooling oven. Leave them undisturbed, without opening the oven door, for 8 to 16 hours.

PLEASE NOTE: Some dogs may be allergic to garlic.

Eggs, Liver & Rice Cookies

Many books on dog nutrition state that most veterinarians recommend that dogs eat eggs, liver, and rice. Well, these cookies combine all three ingredients, and dogs do love them.

$1\frac{1}{2}$ **pounds (about 94 cookies per pound)**

1½ cups whole-wheat flour

1½ cups white corn flour

¾ cup cooked rice

1 pounds raw liver

2 large eggs

beef or chicken broth, or sufficient for processing

1. Position the rack in the center of the oven and preheat at 350ºF. Lightly grease or use parchment paper to line a cookie sheet or baking tray.

2. In a large bowl, using a fork or wire whisk, combine the whole-wheat flour, white corn flour, and rice, stirring until the rice is well separated.

3. In a blender, process the raw liver on HIGH until it turns into a smooth paste. Beat in the eggs until well incorporated.

4. Using a large spoon, a spatula, or your hand, combine the two mixes, blending until the mixture pulls away from the sides of the bowl and forms a soft dough. If the mixture seems a little dry, add a little broth, a tablespoonful at a time.

5. Turn the dough onto a lightly floured flat surface, and using a rolling pin, roll out the dough to $1/4$ inch thick. Use a $1^1/2$-inch round cookie cutter to cut out as many cookies as you can, reworking the scraps as you go. The dough will become stiff as it is reworked.

6. Place the cookies side by side on the prepared cookie sheets or baking trays. Bake for 20 to 25 minutes or until the cookies appear very dry and the edges are light golden brown. Remove the trays from the oven and cool to room temperature. Turn off the oven.

7. When the cookies have cooled completely, put all of them on a single baking tray and return them to the cooling oven. Leave them undisturbed, without opening the oven door, for 8 to 16 hours.

PLEASE NOTE: Some dogs may be allergic to corn-based products.

Cheesy-Cheese dog Treats

Dogs love cheese, and cheese, being a dairy product, is good for them. Cheese is less likely to adversely affect a dog's stomach than, say, something like whole milk. Cottage cheese usually has a bland flavor; that's why I added the grated fresh Romano cheese.

1^1/$_2$ pounds (115 **cookies** per pound)

2 cups whole-wheat flour
^{1}/$_2$ cup soy flour
^{1}/$_4$ cup grated fresh Romano cheese
1 teaspoon garlic powder
1 large egg
^{1}/$_4$ cup canola oil
^{1}/$_2$ cup large-curd cottage cheese
^{2}/$_3$ cup chicken or beef broth

1. Position the rack in the center of the oven and preheat at 350°F. Lightly grease or use parchment paper to line a cookie sheet or baking tray.
2. In a large bowl, using a fork or wire whisk, combine the whole-wheat flour, soy flour, grated cheese, and garlic powder.
3. In a medium bowl, using a wire whisk or electric mixer on MEDIUM speed, beat the egg until foamy. Beat in the oil, and using a large size spoon, stir in the cottage cheese and chicken broth.
4. Using a large spoon, a spatula, or your hand, combine the two mixes, blending until the mixture pulls away from the sides of the bowl and forms a soft dough. If the mixture seems a little dry, add a little broth, a tablespoonful at a time.
5. Turn the dough onto a lightly floured flat surface, and using a rolling pin, roll out to ^{1}/$_4$ inch thick. Use a 1^1/$_2$-inch round cookie cutter to cut out as many cookies as you can, reworking the scraps as you go. The dough will become stiff as it is reworked.

6. Place the cookies side by side on the prepared cookie sheets or baking trays. Bake for 20 to 25 minutes or until the cookies appear very dry and the edges are light golden brown. Remove the trays from the oven and cool to room temperature. Turn off the oven.

7. When the cookies have cooled completely, put all of them on a single baking tray and return them to the cooling oven. Leave them undisturbed, without opening the oven door, for 8 to 16 hours.

PLEASE NOTE: Some dogs may be allergic to garlic, and some dogs may be intolerant of dairy products.

Oatmeal Cookies with Peanut Butter

Few people realize that most dogs love peanut butter. Add to this the distinctively sweet taste of rolled oats and molasses, and you have a cookie that dogs will run a mile to eat.

2 pounds (88 cookies per pound)

3 cups whole-wheat flour

$1/2$ cup uncooked rolled oats

2 teaspoons baking powder

$1^1/2$ cups milk, at room temperature

1 tablespoon molasses

$1^1/4$ cups creamy-style peanut butter

$1/4$ cup chicken broth, or sufficient for processing

1. Position the rack in the center of the oven and preheat at 375°F. Lightly grease or use parchment paper to line two cookie sheets or baking trays.

2. In a large bowl, using a fork or wire whisk, combine the flour, rolled oats, and baking powder.

3. In a medium bowl, using a wire whisk or electric mixer on MEDIUM speed, beat the milk, molasses, and peanut butter together until smooth. Stir in the chicken broth.

4. Using a large spoon, a spatula, or your hand, combine the two mixes, blending until the mixture pulls away from the sides of the bowl and forms a soft dough. If the mixture seems a little dry, add a little broth, a tablespoonful at a time.

5. Turn the dough onto a lightly floured flat surface, and using a rolling pin, roll out to $\frac{1}{4}$ inch thick. Use a $1\frac{1}{2}$-inch round cookie cutter to cut out as many cookies as you can, reworking the scraps as you go. The dough will become stiff as it is reworked.

6. Place the cookies side by side on the prepared cookie sheets or baking trays. Bake for 20 to 25 minutes or until the cookies appear very dry and the edges are light golden brown. Remove the trays from the oven and cool to room temperature. Turn off the oven.

7. When the cookies have cooled completely, put all of them on a single baking tray and return them to the cooling oven. Leave them undisturbed, without opening the oven door, for 8 to 16 hours.

PLEASE NOTE: Some dogs don't tolerate milk.

Sweet Seeds dog Treats

The sweetness comes from the molasses, the seeds from sunflowers, and the recipe from a friend of mine in Japan. This combination is a good one. I don't know if it's the liver or the molasses, but dogs seem to love these treats.

1 1/2 pounds (115 **cookies**)

1 cup unbleached all-purpose flour

1 cup whole-wheat flour

1/4 cup rice flour

1/4 cup desiccated liver

1/2 cup sunflower seeds, crushed (without shells)

2 large eggs

1/4 cup milk, or sufficient for processing

1/4 cup molasses

2 tablespoons canola oil or corn oil

1. Position the rack in the center of the oven and preheat at 350°F. Lightly grease or use parchment paper to line a cookie sheet or baking tray.
2. In a large bowl, using a fork or wire whisk, combine the all-purpose flour, whole-wheat flour, rice flour, liver, and crushed sunflower seeds.
3. In a medium bowl, using a wire whisk or electric mixer on MEDIUM speed, beat the eggs, milk, molasses, and oil together until smooth.
4. Using a large spoon, a spatula, or your hand, combine the two mixes, blending until the mixture pulls away from the sides of the bowl and forms a soft dough. If the mixture seems a little dry, add a little milk, a tablespoonful at a time.
5. Turn the dough onto a lightly floured flat surface, and using a rolling pin, roll out to 1/4 inch thick. Use a 1 1/2-inch round cookie cutter to cut out as many cookies as you can, reworking the scraps as you go. The dough will become stiff as it is reworked.
6. Place the cookies side by side on the prepared cookie sheets or baking trays. Bake for 20

to 25 minutes or until the cookies appear very dry and the edges are light golden brown. Remove the trays from the oven and cool to room temperature. Turn off the oven.

7. When the cookies have cooled completely, put all of them on a single baking tray and return them to the cooling oven. Leave them undisturbed, without opening the oven door, for 8 to 16 hours.

PLEASE NOTE: Some dogs are allergic to corn, and some dogs do not tolerate milk.

doggie stocking stuffers

It is no longer necessary to buy cookies to put in your dog's Christmas stocking. Simply make up a batch of these and you'll have enough cookies to last past New Year's.

$1^3/_4$ to 2 pounds (143 **cookies** per pound)

2 cups whole-wheat flour

1 cup unbleached all-purpose flour

1 cup graham flour

1 cup soy flour

$^3/_4$ pound raw chicken livers

$^1/_4$ cup beef or chicken broth, or sufficient for processing

$^1/_4$ cup canola oil or corn oil

1 large egg

1. Position the rack in the center of the oven and preheat at 350°F. Lightly grease or use parchment paper to line a cookie sheet or baking tray.
2. In a large bowl, using a fork or wire whisk, combine the four flours.

3. In a blender, process the chicken livers on HIGH until they become a smooth paste. Beat in the broth, oil, and egg, continuing to process until smooth.

4. Using a large spoon, a spatula, or your hand, combine the two mixes, blending until the mixture pulls away from the sides of the bowl and forms a soft dough. If the mixture seems a little dry, add a little broth, a tablespoonful at a time.

5. Turn the dough onto a lightly floured flat surface, and using a rolling pin, roll out to $^1/_4$ inch thick. Use a $1^1/_2$-inch round cookie cutter to cut out as many cookies as you can, reworking the scraps as you go. The dough will become stiff as it is reworked.

6. Place the cookies side by side on the prepared cookie sheets or baking trays. Bake for 15 to 20 minutes or until the cookies appear very dry and the edges are light golden brown. Remove the trays from the oven and cool to room temperature. Turn off the oven.

7. When the cookies have cooled completely, put all of them on a single baking tray and return them to the cooling oven. Leave them undisturbed, without opening the oven door, for 8 to 16 hours.

PLEASE NOTE: Some dogs may be allergic to corn-based products. If so, use canola oil instead of corn oil.

Little Liver Squares

Here's another easy dog-cookie recipe. These cookie squares are good and nutritious.

1½ pounds (112 **cookies** per pound)

1 pound raw beef liver or pork liver

4 large eggs

½ cup yellow cornmeal

1 cup white corn flour

½ cup soy flour

¼ teaspoon garlic powder

¼ cup beef or chicken broth, or sufficient for processing

1. Position the rack in the center of the oven and preheat at 400°F. Lightly grease or use parchment paper to line a 13 x 10 x 1½-inch baking pan.

2. In a blender, process the liver on HIGH speed until smooth. Continue beating and add the eggs one at a time.

3. In a large bowl, using a fork or wire whisk, combine the cornmeal, white corn flour, soy flour, and garlic powder.

4. Using a large spoon, a spatula, or your hand, combine the two mixes, blending until the mixture pulls away from the sides of the bowl and forms a soft dough. If the mixture seems a little dry, add a little broth, a tablespoonful at a time.

5. Spread the dough evenly into the prepared baking pan. Bake for about 20 to 25 minutes or until the cookies appear very dry and the edges are light golden brown. Remove the trays from the oven and, immediately using a pizza cutter or small spatula, cut the cake into as many small squares as you think you'll need. Turn off the oven and cool the cookies to room temperature.

6. When the cookies have cooled completely, put all of them on a single baking tray and return them to the cooling oven. Leave them undisturbed, without opening the oven door, for 8 to 16 hours.

PLEASE NOTE: Some dogs may be allergic to corn-based products or garlic.

Beef-Flavored Canine Cookies

Unlike so many dog cookies, these treats rise. During baking they may become a little puffy; this is normal.

1¼ pounds (125 **cookies** per pound)

3 cups whole-wheat flour

½ cup unbleached all-purpose flour

1½ teaspoons baking powder

2 tablespoons crisp cooked bacon, crumbled

¼ cup vegetable shortening

4.5-ounce jar beef-flavored baby food

2 large eggs

¼ cup beef or chicken broth, or sufficient for processing

1. Position the rack in the center of the oven and preheat at 350°F. Lightly grease or use parchment paper to line a cookie sheet or baking tray.
2. In a large bowl, using a fork or wire whisk, combine the whole-wheat flour, all-purpose flour, baking powder, and bacon. Using a pastry blender or two knives, cut in the shortening until the mixture resembles fine crumbs.
3. In a medium bowl, using a wire whisk or electric mixer on MEDIUM speed, beat together the baby food, eggs, and broth.
4. Using a large spoon, a spatula, or your hand, combine the two mixes, blending until the mixture pulls away from the sides of the bowl and forms a soft dough. If the mixture seems a little dry, add a little broth, a tablespoonful at a time.
5. Turn the dough onto a lightly floured flat surface, and using a rolling pin, roll out to ¼ inch thick. Use a 1½-inch round cookie cutter to cut out as many cookies as you can, reworking the scraps as you go. The dough will become stiff as it is reworked.
6. Place the cookies side by side on the prepared cookie sheet or baking tray. Bake for 20 to 25 minutes or until the cookies appear very dry and the edges are light golden brown. Remove the tray from the oven and cool to room temperature. Turn off the oven.

7. When the cookies have cooled completely, put all of them on a single baking tray and return them to the cooling oven. Leave them undisturbed, without opening the oven door, for 8 to 16 hours.

Western Buckwheat dog Biscuits

Because buckwheat is such a strong flour, these cookies have a moderately aggressive taste. This also means that the baby-food flavor does not become the overpowering flavoring it could be.

1¹/₂ to 2 pounds (114 cookies per pound)

> 2 cups whole-wheat flour
> ¹/₂ cup buckwheat flour
> ¹/₂ cup wheat bran
> ¹/₂ cup nonfat dry milk powder
> 1 large egg
> 2.5-ounce jar beef-flavored baby food
> ¹/₄ cup beef or chicken broth, or sufficient for processing

1. Position the rack in the center of the oven and preheat at 400°F. Lightly grease or use parchment paper to line two cookie sheets or baking trays.
2. In a large bowl, using a fork or wire whisk, blend the whole-wheat flour, buckwheat flour, bran, and dry milk.
3. In a medium bowl, using a wire whisk or electric mixer on MEDIUM speed, beat together the egg, baby food, and broth.

Tasty Treats for Demanding Dogs

4. Using a large spoon, a spatula, or your hand, combine the two mixes, blending until the mixture pulls away from the sides of the bowl and forms a soft dough. If the mixture seems a little dry, add a little broth, a tablespoonful at a time.

5. Turn the dough onto a lightly floured flat surface, and using a rolling pin, roll out to $1/4$ inch thick. Use a $1^1/_2$-inch round cookie cutter to cut out as many cookies as you can, reworking the scraps as you go. The dough will become stiff as it is reworked.

6. Place the cookies side by side on the prepared cookie sheets or baking trays. Bake for 20 to 25 minutes or until the cookies appear very dry and the edges are light golden brown. Remove the trays from the oven and cool to room temperature. Turn off the oven.

7. When the cookies have cooled completely, put all of them on a single baking tray and return them to the cooling oven. Leave them undisturbed, without opening the oven door, for 8 to 16 hours.

PLEASE NOTE: Some dogs may not tolerate milk.

Chick-a-dee dog Biscuits

I've never met a dog that didn't like chicken, although I've known a few that were not too fond of turkey. The chicken livers make this an exceptional treat for dogs.

1 to 1½ pounds (135 **cookies** per pound)

2 cups whole-wheat flour

½ cup wheat germ

½ cup oat bran

1 tablespoon fresh parsley

1 large egg

¼ cup canola oil or corn oil

1 cup raw chicken livers

¾ cup chicken broth or drippings, or sufficient for processing

1. Position the rack in the center of the oven and preheat at 400°F. Lightly grease or use parchment paper to line two cookie sheets or baking trays.
2. In a large bowl, using a fork or wire whisk, blend the flour, wheat germ, oat bran, and parsley.
3. In a blender, combine the egg, oil, chicken livers, and chicken broth, processing on HIGH until smooth.
4. Using a large spoon, a spatula, or your hand, combine the two mixes, blending until the mixture pulls away from the sides of the bowl and forms a soft dough. If the mixture seems a little dry, add broth, a tablespoonful at a time.
5. Turn the dough onto a lightly floured flat surface, and using a rolling pin, roll out to ¼ inch thick. Use a 1½-inch round cookie cutter to cut out as many cookies as you can, reworking the scraps as you go. The dough will become stiff as it is reworked.
6. Place the cookies side by side on the prepared cookie sheets or baking trays. Bake for 20 to 25 minutes or until the cookies appear very dry and the edges are light golden

brown. Remove the trays from the oven and cool to room temperature. Turn off the oven.

7. When the cookies have cooled completely, put all of them on a single baking tray and return them to the cooling oven. Leave them undisturbed, without opening the oven door, for 8 to 16 hours.

PLEASE NOTE: Some dogs may be allergic to corn-based products. If yours is, use canola oil instead of corn oil.

doggie Nibble Bars

The easy part of making these treats for dogs is that the dough doesn't have to be rolled out. Here the dough is pressed into a baking pan or tray and baked. After baking, simply cut them into small squares or triangles.

1 to 1½ pounds (30 to 32 **bars** per pound)

$1/4$ cup whole-wheat flour

$1/2$ cup soy flour

2 cups dry beef-flavored kibble dog food, finely ground

$1/4$ pound cooked lean ground beef, finely minced

1 large egg

$1/4$ cup honey

$1/4$ cup canola oil or corn oil

1. Position the rack in the center of the oven and preheat at 350ºF. Lightly grease or use parchment paper to line a $10^{1}/_{2}$ x $7^{1}/_{2}$ x $1^{1}/_{2}$-inch baking pan.

2. In a large bowl, using a fork or wire whisk, blend the whole-wheat flour, soy flour, kibble dog food, and ground beef.

3. In a small bowl, using a wire whisk or electric mixer on MEDIUM speed, beat together the egg, honey, and oil.

4. Using a large spoon, a spatula, or your hands, combine the two mixes, blending until the mixture pulls away from the sides of the bowl and forms into a sticky dough.

5. Press the dough evenly into the bottom of the prepared baking pan, and using a floured knife, score deep lines into the dough, seven lines across and four lines lengthwise.

6. Bake for about 15 to 20 minutes, or until the top becomes a dusty brown and an inserted toothpick is removed clean. Remove the pan from the oven, and invert it onto a wire rack to cool completely.

7. Remove the pan and break the cookies into the small squares previously laid out by scoring.

8. Place the cookies back on a cookie sheet, and with the oven off, return the cookies to the cooling oven for at least 8 hours or overnight. Place them in a covered container.

> **PLEASE NOTE:** Some dogs may be allergic to corn-based products.

Cheese Biscuits

Your favorite four-legged friend will greedily accept these biscuits. Some cheeses are tart or sweet, others are dry, and still others are moist. You can vary the taste by varying the type of cheese you use. The only requisite is that you should be able to grate the cheese.

2 to 2$^1\!/_2$ pounds (133 cookies per pound)

3$^1\!/_2$ cups whole-wheat flour

1 cup uncooked rolled oats

1 cup yellow cornmeal

$^1\!/_2$ cup nonfat dry milk

1 cup wheat bran

1 cup grated cheddar cheese

2 large eggs

1$\frac{1}{2}$ cups chicken broth, or sufficient for processing

1. Position the rack in the center of the oven and preheat at 400°F. Lightly grease or use parchment paper to line two cookie sheets or baking trays.

2. In a large bowl, using a fork or wire whisk, blend the flour, oats, cornmeal, dry milk, wheat bran, and cheddar cheese.

3. In a small bowl, using a wire whisk or electric mixer on MEDIUM speed, beat the eggs foamy before beating in the chicken broth.

4. Using a large spoon, a spatula, or your hand, combine the two mixes, blending until the mixture pulls away from the sides of the bowl and forms a soft dough. If the mixture seems a little dry, add a little broth, a tablespoonful at a time.

5. Turn the dough onto a lightly floured flat surface, and using a rolling pin, roll out to $\frac{1}{4}$ inch thick. Use a 1$\frac{1}{2}$-inch round cookie cutter to cut out as many cookies as you can, reworking the scraps as you go. The dough will become stiff as it is reworked.

6. Place the cookies side by side on the prepared cookie sheets or baking trays. Bake for 20 to 25 minutes or until the cookies appear very dry and the edges are light golden brown. Remove the trays from the oven and cool to room temperature. Turn off the oven.

7. When the cookies have cooled completely, put all of them on a single baking tray and return them to the cooling oven. Leave them undisturbed, without opening the oven door, for 8 to 16 hours.

   PLEASE NOTE: Some dogs may be allergic to corn-based products or sensitive to dairy products.

dog's soupy Treats

Few people have ever thought of making cookies using soup. Since there's a lot of nutritional benefit in most commercially prepared soups, why not use them? Remember that the quality of the chosen soup will determine the quality of the treat.

1 to 1^1/$_2$ pounds (90 **cookies** per pound)

2 cups whole-wheat flour

2 cups all-purpose flour

^{1}/$_2$ cup cracked-wheat flakes

2 large eggs

10.5-ounce can cream-of-chicken soup, undiluted

2 tablespoons canola oil or corn oil

^{1}/$_3$ cup chicken broth or fresh drippings, or sufficient for processing

1. Position the rack in the center of the oven and preheat at 350°F. Lightly grease or use parchment paper to line two cookie sheets or baking trays.
2. In a large bowl, using a fork or wire whisk, blend the whole-wheat flour, all-purpose flour, and cracked-wheat flakes.
3. In a medium bowl, using a wire whisk or electric mixer on MEDIUM speed, beat together the eggs, soup, oil, and broth.
4. Using a large spoon, a spatula, or your hand, combine the two mixes, blending until the mixture pulls away from the sides of the bowl and forms a soft dough. If the mixture seems a little dry, add a little broth, a tablespoonful at a time.
5. Turn the dough onto a lightly floured flat surface, and using a rolling pin, roll out to ^{1}/$_4$ inch thick. Use a 1^1/$_2$-inch round cookie cutter to cut out as many cookies as you can, reworking the scraps as you go. The dough will become stiff as it is reworked.
6. Place the cookies side by side on the prepared cookie sheets or baking trays. Bake for 20 to 25 minutes or until the cookies appear very dry and the edges are light golden

brown. Remove the trays from the oven and cool to room temperature. Turn off the oven.

7. When the cookies have cooled completely, put all of them on a single baking tray and return them to the cooling oven. Leave them undisturbed, without opening the oven door, for 8 to 16 hours.

PLEASE NOTE: Some dogs may be allergic to corn-based products or sensitive to dairy products.

Chickie do's

These treats combine chicken with a carrot-and-cheese taste.

1 to 1¹/₂ pounds (133 **cookies** per pound)

1¹/₂ cups whole-wheat flour

¹/₂ pound cooked ground chicken, finely minced

1 large carrot, scraped and finely grated

1 teaspoon Romano or Parmesan cheese, grated

¹/₄ teaspoon garlic powder

2 large eggs

1 tablespoon processed cheese spread

¹/₂ cup chicken broth, or sufficient for processing

1. Position the rack in the center of the oven and preheat at 400ºF. Lightly grease or use parchment paper to line two cookie sheets or baking trays.
2. In a large bowl, using a fork or wire whisk, blend the flour, chicken, carrot, cheese, and garlic powder.
3. In a small bowl, using a fork or wire whisk, blend the eggs, cheese spread, and chicken broth until smooth.

4. Using a large spoon, a spatula, or your hand, combine the two mixes, blending until the mixture pulls away from the sides of the bowl and forms a soft dough. If the mixture seems a little dry, add a little broth, a tablespoonful at a time.

5. Turn the dough onto a lightly floured flat surface, and using a rolling pin, roll out to $1/4$ inch thick. Use a $1^{1}/_{2}$-inch round cookie cutter to cut out as many cookies as you can, reworking the scraps as you go. The dough will become stiff as it is reworked.

6. Place the cookies side by side on the prepared cookie sheets or baking trays. Bake for 20 to 25 minutes or until the cookies appear very dry and the edges are light golden brown. Remove the trays from the oven and cool to room temperature. Turn off the oven.

7. When the cookies have cooled completely, put all of them on a single baking tray and return them to the cooling oven. Leave them undisturbed, without opening the oven door, for 8 to 16 hours.

PLEASE NOTE: Some dogs may be allergic to garlic or sensitive to dairy products.

Chicken & Cheese Treats

Some pampered dogs like chicken, and some like turkey. You can use either fowl in this recipe.

1 to 1$^{1}/_{4}$ pounds (125 **cookies** per pound)

$2^{1}/_{2}$ cups whole-wheat flour

$^{1}/_{2}$ cup bleached all-purpose flour

$^{1}/_{2}$ cup wheat flakes

1 tablespoon brewer's yeast

2 tablespoons hard cheese, grated

$^{1}/_{2}$ pound cooked chicken livers, chopped very fine *or* $^{1}/_{2}$ pound ground turkey, cooked and finely minced

WOW

1 large egg

2 tablespoons canola oil or corn oil

$1/2$ cup chicken broth or drippings

hard, grated cheese for sprinkling

1. Position the rack in the center of the oven and preheat at 400°F. Lightly grease or use parchment paper to line two cookie sheets or baking trays.

2. In a large bowl, using a fork or wire whisk, blend the whole-wheat flour, all-purpose flour, wheat flakes, yeast, cheese, and chicken livers.

3. In a small bowl, using a fork or wire whisk, beat together the egg, oil, and broth until smooth.

4. Using a large spoon, a spatula, or your hand, combine the two mixes, blending until the mixture pulls away from the sides of the bowl and forms a soft dough. If the mixture seems a little dry, add a little broth, a tablespoonful at a time.

5. Turn the dough onto a lightly floured flat surface, and using a rolling pin, roll out to $1/4$ inch thick. Use a $1^{1}/2$-inch round cookie cutter to cut out as many cookies as you can, reworking the scraps as you go. The dough will become stiff as it is reworked.

6. Place the cookies side by side on the prepared cookie sheets or baking trays and sprinkle them with a little cheese. Bake for 20 to 25 minutes or until the cookies appear very dry and the edges are light golden brown. Remove the trays from the oven and cool to room temperature. Turn off the oven.

7. When the cookies have cooled completely, put all of them on a single baking tray and return them to the cooling oven. Leave them undisturbed, without opening the oven door, for 8 to 16 hours.

    PLEASE NOTE: Some dogs may be allergic to corn-based products or sensitive to dairy products.

Chicken-Gizzard Treats

Other than gravy or the occasional snack food, there are very few uses for chicken gizzards. This is one use that pays off with dividends.

$1^3/_4$ to 2 pounds (146 **cookies** per pound)

1 cup rye flour

$1^1/_2$ cups whole-wheat flour

1 cup unbleached all-purpose flour

$^1/_2$ cup nonfat dry milk

6 tablespoons vegetable shortening

1 pound cooked chicken gizzards, minced very fine

1 large egg

$1^1/_2$ cup chicken broth or drippings, or sufficient for processing

1. Position the rack in the center of the oven and preheat at 400°F. Lightly grease or use parchment paper to line two cookie sheets or baking trays.
2. In a large bowl, using a fork or wire whisk, blend the rye flour, whole-wheat flour, all-purpose flour, and dry milk. Using a pastry blender or two knives, cut in the shortening until the mixture resembles fine crumbs. Stir in the chicken.
3. In a small bowl, using a fork or wire whisk, beat together the egg and broth.
4. Using a large spoon, a spatula, or your hand, combine the two mixes, blending until the mixture pulls away from the sides of the bowl and forms a soft dough. If the mixture seems a little dry, add a little broth, a tablespoonful at a time.
5. Turn the dough onto a lightly floured flat surface, and using a rolling pin, roll out to $^1/_4$ inch thick. Use a $1^1/_2$-inch round cookie cutter to cut out as many cookies as you can, reworking the scraps as you go. The dough will become stiff as it is reworked.
6. Place the cookies side by side on the prepared cookie sheets or baking trays. Bake for 20 to 25 minutes or until the cookies appear very dry and the edges are light golden

brown. Remove the trays from the oven and cool to room temperature. Turn off the oven.

7. When the cookies have cooled completely, put all of them on a single baking tray and return them to the cooling oven. Leave them undisturbed, without opening the oven door, for 8 to 16 hours.

PLEASE NOTE: Some dogs may be sensitive to dairy products.

Familiar dog Treats

In a dog's life, the food you feed him every day becomes familiar. If you store your dog's favorite treats in a can, jar, box, or other container, he will soon recognize the source and associate the container with these great treats.

$1^1/_2$ to $1^3/_4$ pounds (102 **cookies** per pound)

$1^1/_2$ cups whole-wheat flour

1 cup unbleached all-purpose flour

0.25-ounce package unflavored gelatin (Knox® or generic)

1 cup nonfat dry milk

1 tablespoon brewer's yeast

1 large egg

1 tablespoon honey

$^1/_4$ cup canola oil or corn oil

6-ounce can prepared dog food (not chunky style), crumbled

$^1/_4$ cup beef or chicken broth, or sufficient for processing

1. Position the rack in the center of the oven and preheat at 400°F. Lightly grease or use parchment paper to line two cookie sheets or baking trays.

2. In a large bowl, using a fork or wire whisk, blend the two flours, gelatin, dry milk, and yeast.

3. In a medium bowl, using a wire whisk or electric mixer on MEDIUM speed, beat the egg until foamy; then beat in the honey, oil, dog food, and broth.

4. Using a large spoon, a spatula, or your hand, combine the two mixes, blending until the mixture pulls away from the sides of the bowl and forms a soft dough. If the mixture seems a little dry, add a little broth, a tablespoonful at a time.

5. Turn the dough onto a lightly floured flat surface, and using a rolling pin, roll out to $1/4$ inch thick. Use a $1^{1/2}$-inch round cookie cutter to cut out as many cookies as you can, reworking the scraps as you go. The dough will become stiff as it is reworked.

6. Place the cookies side by side on the prepared cookie sheets or baking trays. Bake for 20 to 25 minutes or until the cookies appear very dry and the edges are light golden brown. Remove the trays from the oven and cool to room temperature. Turn off the oven.

7. When the cookies have cooled completely, put all of them on a single baking tray and return them to the cooling oven. Leave them undisturbed, without opening the oven door, for 8 to 16 hours.

PLEASE NOTE: Some dogs may be sensitive to dairy products.

Easy doggie strips

We love our dogs, and we like to give them treats we know they'll eat and enjoy. Unfortunately, the most popular—jerky for dogs—is very expensive. This simplified method of making meat strips works pretty well.

¹/₂ to ³/₄ pound strips

6 to 8 hot dogs or frankfurters
¹/₂ cup beef drippings

1. Using a very sharp knife or a cheese or butter cutter (the kind with a taut wire), slice the hot dogs into as many thin slices as possible. A cheese or butter cutter will create the most even slices.
2. Arrange the slices in a shallow pan or bowl and pour the drippings over the top. Set aside for at least one hour or overnight.
3. Place them on a microwave-proof plate or platter and microwave on HIGH for 3 minutes. Remove from the microwave and cool to room temperature, about 5 minutes. Then return them to the oven and microwave on HIGH again for another 3 minutes.
4. Remove from the oven and repeat until the slices have reached the jerky stage of dryness. Be sure to allow for cooling time in between each cooking.
5. Store in an airtight container in the refrigerator.
6. Baking note: These strips can also be made with sausage, although they will have to be sliced with a meat slicer or knife.

PLEASE NOTE: Some hot dogs or frankfurters may contain undesirable additives.

Woof Balls

These delicious balls make a great treat for dogs. You can feed them to your four-legged friend liberally. They're not cookies, so be sure to store these meaty balls in the refrigerator after cooking them.

2 to 2¼ pounds balls

1½ pounds high-fat-content ground beef

¼ pound high-fat-content ground pork

3 cups quick rolled oats

½ cup wheat germ

¼ cup desiccated bone meal

4 teaspoons molasses

4 large egg yolks

1. In a medium bowl, using a fork or your hands, blend the beef and pork.
2. In a large bowl, using a fork or wire whisk, blend the rolled oats, wheat germ, and bone meal.
3. In a small bowl, using a fork, beat together the molasses and egg yolks.
4. Using a large spoon, fork, or your hands, combine the three mixes, blending until thoroughly incorporated. Flour your hands and pinch off pieces of the dough, about the size of small olives, and form them into balls.
5. Place them on a microwave-proof plate or platter lined with parchment paper, and microwave on HIGH for 3 minutes. Remove from the microwave and cool to room temperature. Return to the oven and microwave for another 3 minutes.
6. Remove from the oven, cool to room temperature, and transfer to a refrigerator storage container. Store them in the refrigerator. They'll keep about 7 to 10 days in the refrigerator and longer in the freezer.

Chicken Biscuits

Dogs go for these because of the chicken. But they come back for seconds and thirds because of the yeast, oat bran, and graham flour. Like all my recipes, they're easy to make and add a bit of variety to other dog treats you have been feeding your pet.

2$\frac{1}{3}$ to 3 pounds (139 **cookies** per pound)

$3\frac{1}{4}$ cups unbleached all-purpose flour

2 cups whole-wheat flour

$\frac{1}{2}$ cup graham flour

1 cup oat bran

1 cup cracked wheat

$\frac{1}{2}$ cup nonfat dry milk

1 tablespoon brewer's yeast

$\frac{1}{3}$ cup raw chicken livers

2 cups chicken broth, or sufficient for processing

1 large egg

1. Position the rack in the center of the oven and preheat at 400°F. Lightly grease or use parchment paper to line two cookie sheets or baking trays.
2. In a large bowl, using a fork or wire whisk, blend the all-purpose flour, whole-wheat flour, and graham flour with the oat bran, cracked wheat, dry milk, and yeast.
3. In a blender, combine the chicken liver, broth, and egg. Process on HIGH until smooth.
4. Using a large spoon, a spatula, or your hand, combine the two mixes, blending until the mixture pulls away from the sides of the bowl and forms a soft dough. If the mixture seems a little dry, add a little broth, a tablespoonful at a time.
5. Turn the dough onto a lightly floured flat surface, and using a rolling pin, roll out to $\frac{1}{4}$ inch thick. Use a $1\frac{1}{2}$-inch round cookie cutter to cut out as many cookies as you can, reworking the scraps as you go. The dough will become stiff as it is reworked.

6. Place the cookies side by side on the prepared cookie sheets or baking trays. Bake for 15 to 18 minutes or until the cookies appear very dry and the edges are light golden brown. Remove the trays from the oven and cool to room temperature. Turn off the oven.

7. When the cookies have cooled completely, put all of them on a single baking tray and return them to the cooling oven. Leave them undisturbed, without opening the oven door, for 8 to 16 hours.

PLEASE NOTE: Some dogs may be sensitive to dairy products.

Simplest dog Biscuits

This recipe represents just about the easiest kind of baked dog cookies that can be made. Most kitchens stock these basic ingredients.

1 to 1¼ pounds (100 **cookies** per pound)

3 cups whole-wheat flour

½ cup nonfat dry milk

⅓ cup vegetable shortening

1 large egg

¾ cup beef or chicken broth, or sufficient for processing

1. Position the rack in the center of the oven and preheat at 400°F. Lightly grease or use parchment paper to line two cookie sheets or baking trays.

2. In a large bowl, using a fork or wire whisk, blend the flour and dry milk. Using a pastry blender or two knives, cut in the shortening.

3. In a small bowl, using a fork, beat the egg and broth together until smooth.

4. Using a large spoon, a spatula, or your hand, combine the two mixes, blending until the

mixture pulls away from the sides of the bowl and a soft sticky dough forms. If the mixture seems a little dry, add a little broth, a tablespoonful at a time.

5. Turn the dough onto a lightly floured flat surface, and using a rolling pin, roll out to $\frac{1}{4}$ inch thick. Use a $1\frac{1}{2}$-inch round cookie cutter to cut out as many cookies as you can, reworking the scraps as you go. The dough will become stiff as it is reworked.

6. Place the cookies side by side on the prepared cookie sheets or baking trays. Bake for 20 to 25 minutes or until the cookies appear very dry and the edges are light golden brown. Remove the trays from the oven and cool to room temperature. Turn off the oven.

7. When the cookies have cooled completely, put all of them on a single baking tray and return them to the cooling oven. Leave them undisturbed, without opening the oven door, for 8 to 16 hours.

PLEASE NOTE: Some dogs may be sensitive to dairy products.

Chicken-Liver Treats

Does your dog like chicken? If he does, here's one of many treats using chicken livers and chicken broth as flavors and ingredients.

1½ to 1¾ pounds (144 **cookies** per pound)

> 1 pound raw chicken liver
>
> 1 cup vegetable shortening, at room temperature
>
> ½ cup nonfat dry milk
>
> 1 cup chicken broth or drippings, or sufficient for processing
>
> 4 cups unbleached all-purpose flour
>
> ¼ cup soy flour

1. Position the rack in the center of the oven and preheat at 400°F. Lightly grease or use parchment paper to line two cookie sheets or baking trays.

2. In a blender, combine the livers, shortening, dry milk, and chicken broth. Process on HIGH until the mixture is smooth.

3. In a large bowl, using a fork or wire whisk, blend the two flours.

4. Using a large spoon, a spatula, or your hand, combine the two mixes, blending until the mixture pulls away from the sides of the bowl and forms a soft dough. If the mixture seems a little dry, add a little broth, a tablespoonful at a time.

5. Turn the dough onto a lightly floured flat surface, and using a rolling pin, roll out to ¼ inch thick. Use a 1½-inch round cookie cutter to cut out as many cookies as you can, reworking the scraps as you go. The dough will become stiff as it is reworked.

6. Place the cookies side by side on the prepared cookie sheets or baking trays. Bake for 20 to 25 minutes or until the cookies appear very dry and the edges are light golden brown. Remove trays from the oven and cool to room temperature. Turn off the oven.

7. When the cookies have cooled completely, put all of them on a single baking tray and return them to the cooling oven. Leave them undisturbed, without opening the oven door, for 8 to 16 hours.

   PLEASE NOTE: Some dogs may be sensitive to dairy products.

Canine Cookies

The chicken-soup baby food provides the dominant flavor. During testing, it was a surprise that not one dog refused them, and what's more important, not one spat them out. All the dogs ate them.

$3/4$ to 1 pounds (90 **cookies** per pound)

2 cups whole-wheat flour

$1/2$ **cup unbleached all-purpose flour**

$1/2$ **cup nonfat dry milk or whey powder**

$1/2$ **teaspoon garlic powder**

1 large egg

1 tablespoon molasses (optional)

4.5-ounce jar chicken-soup baby food

$3/4$ **cup chicken broth or drippings, or sufficient for processing**

1. Position the rack in the center of the oven and preheat at 400°F. Lightly grease or use parchment paper to line two cookie sheets or baking trays.
2. In a large bowl, using a fork or wire whisk, blend the whole-wheat flour, all-purpose flour, dry milk, and garlic powder.
3. In a medium bowl, using a wire whisk or electric mixer on MEDIUM speed, beat the egg until foamy before beating in the molasses, baby food, and broth.
4. Using a large spoon, a spatula, or your hand, combine the two mixes, blending until the mixture pulls away from the sides of the bowl and forms a soft dough. If the mixture seems a little dry, add a little broth, a tablespoonful at a time.
5. Turn the dough onto a lightly floured flat surface, and using a rolling pin, roll out to $1/4$ inch thick. Use a $1^1/2$-inch round cookie cutter to cut out as many cookies as you can, reworking the scraps as you go. The dough will become stiff as it is reworked.
6. Place the cookies side by side on the prepared cookie sheets or baking trays. Bake for 15 to 20 minutes or until the cookies appear very dry and the edges are light golden

brown. Remove the trays from the oven and cool to room temperature. Turn off the oven.

7. When the cookies have cooled completely, put all of them on a single baking tray and return them to the cooling oven. Leave them undisturbed, without opening the oven door, for 8 to 16 hours.

PLEASE NOTE: Some dogs may be allergic to garlic or sensitive to dairy products.

Vegetable-Flavored doggie Cookies

Since some vegetarians try to get their dogs to follow a vegetarian regime, I've included this recipe for them. However, I must add that relatively few dogs would accept this cookie. Dogs require meat protein to stay healthy.

1 pound (98 **cookies** per pound)

1 cup finely crushed dried bread crumbs

1 cup unbleached whole-wheat flour

1 cup bulgur wheat

$^1/_4$ cup soy milk

$1^1/_2$ teaspoons brewer's yeast

1 cup vegetable stock, or sufficient for processing

1. Position the rack in the center of the oven and preheat at 400°F. Lightly grease or use parchment paper to line two cookie sheets or baking trays.

2. In a large bowl, using a fork or wire whisk, blend the bread crumbs, flour, wheat, soy milk, and yeast.

3. Using a fork, make an indentation in the center of the dry mix and add 1 cup of stock.

4. Using a large spoon, a spatula, or your hand, blend until the mixture pulls away from the sides of the bowl and forms a soft dough. If the mixture seems a little dry, add a little stock, a tablespoonful at a time.

5. Turn the dough onto a lightly floured flat surface, and using a rolling pin, roll out to $\frac{1}{4}$ inch thick. Use a $1\frac{1}{2}$-inch round cookie cutter to cut out as many cookies as you can, reworking the scraps as you go. The dough will become stiff as it is reworked.

6. Place the cookies side by side on the prepared cookie sheets or baking trays. Bake for 20 to 25 minutes or until the cookies appear very dry and the edges are light golden brown. Remove the trays from the oven and cool to room temperature. Turn off the oven.

7. When the cookies have cooled completely, put all of them on a single baking tray and return them to the cooling oven. Leave them undisturbed, without opening the oven door, for 8 to 16 hours.

15-Minute dog Cookies

Over the past 30 years, I have seen a large number of recipes for dog cookies, but these seem to be the fastest to make and bake.

³/₄ pound (132 cookies per pound)

1 cup whole-wheat flour

³/₄ cup nonfat dry milk

¹/₂ cup quick oatmeal

¹/₄ cup yellow cornmeal

¹/₃ cup vegetable shortening

1 large egg

¹/₂ cup beef or chicken broth, or sufficient for processing

1. In a large bowl, using a fork or wire whisk, blend the flour, dry milk, oatmeal, and cornmeal. Using two knives or a pastry blender, cut in the shortening until fine crumbs form.

2. In a small bowl, using a wire whisk, or electric mixer on MEDIUM speed, beat together the egg and broth.

3. Using a large spoon, a spatula, or your hand, combine the two mixes, blending until the mixture pulls away from the sides of the bowl and forms a soft dough. If the mixture seems a little dry, add a little broth, a tablespoonful at a time.

4. Turn the dough onto a lightly floured flat surface, and using a rolling pin, roll out to ¹/₄ inch thick. Use a 1¹/₂-inch round cookie cutter to cut out as many cookies as you can, reworking the scraps as you go. The dough will become stiff as it is reworked.

5. Place the cookies side by side on a microwave-proof dish or tray, and cook on LOW for 5 to 10 minutes. Remove from the oven and cool to room temperature.

PLEASE NOTE: Some dogs may be allergic to corn-based products or sensitive to dairy products.

 100 **Tasty Treats for Demanding Dogs**

dog sticks

My dogs are particularly happy when I make these. They play with these sticks; one dog tries to take a stick from the other. So they have fun before eating them and are eager to come back for more. These dog sticks take a little more work than other treats, but they're well worth it.

1 to 1½ pounds (10 sticks per pound)

3 cups whole-wheat flour

½ cup nonfat dry milk

⅓ cup vegetable shortening

1 large egg

¾ cup fresh beef, pork, or lamb drippings, or sufficient for processing

1. Position the rack in the center of the oven and preheat at 350°F. Lightly grease or use parchment paper to line two cookie sheets or baking trays.
2. In a large bowl, using a fork or wire whisk, blend the flour and dry milk.
3. Using a pastry blender or two knives, cut in the shortening until the mixture resembles fine meal.
4. In a small bowl, using a fork, beat the egg slightly before adding the drippings.
5. Using a large spoon, a spatula, or your hand, blend until the mixture pulls away from the sides of the bowl and forms a soft dough. If the mixture seems a little dry, add a little of the drippings, a tablespoonful at a time.
6. Turn the dough onto a lightly floured flat surface, and knead several times. Pinch off pieces about the size of a large walnut, and rolling the dough between your hands, form into a log about the thickness of a cigar.
7. Place the logs on the prepared baking trays. Bake for about 20 to 25 minutes or until the logs appear to dry out and are light golden brown. Remove them from the oven and cool to room temperature. Turn off the oven.

8. When the cookies have cooled completely, put all of them on a single baking tray and return them to the cooling oven. Leave them undisturbed, without opening the oven door, for 8 to 16 hours.

PLEASE NOTE: Some dogs may be sensitive to dairy products.

Bacon & Liver Treats

Bacon fat is one of the best fats you can give a dog, and liver has wondrous properties that we're still finding out about. Combine the two ingredients, and not only is this a cookie dogs will eat, but it's a cookie that's good for them.

3½ pounds (12 to 14 **cookies** per pound)

3½ cups whole-wheat flour

½ cup nonfat dry milk

½ cup chilled bacon drippings

2 tablespoons desiccated liver

3 cups quick rolled oats

2 large eggs

1½ cups beef or chicken broth or drippings, or sufficient for processing

1. Position the rack in the center of the oven and preheat at 400°F. Lightly grease or use parchment paper to line two cookie sheets or baking trays.
2. In a large bowl, using a fork or wire whisk, blend the flour and dry milk.
3. Using a pastry blender or two knives, cut in the bacon drippings until the mixture resembles fine meal. Using a fork, stir in the liver and oats.
4. In a medium bowl, using a wire whisk or electric mixer on MEDIUM speed, beat the eggs until foamy before beating in the broth.

5. Using a large spoon, a spatula, or your hand, blend until the mixture pulls away from the sides of the bowl and a soft, somewhat sticky dough forms.

6. Using a teaspoon, drop heaping spoonfuls of the mixture $1/2$ inch apart onto the prepared baking trays. Bake for 20 to 25 minutes or until the cookies appear very dry and the edges are light golden brown. Remove the trays from the oven and cool to room temperature. Turn off the oven.

7. When the cookies have cooled completely, put all of them on a single baking tray and return them to the cooling oven. Leave them undisturbed, without opening the oven door, for 8 to 16 hours.

PLEASE NOTE: Some dogs are sensitive to dairy products.

Cheesy Rings

These rings can be a great source of amusement for your dog. You can play fetch with them. They're easy to toss and can be eaten after play. The size of the cheesy ring should fit your dog's mouth. Make large rings for large dogs and small rings for small dogs.

$1^{1}/_{2}$ to 2 pounds (12 **rings** per pound)

$3^{3}/_{4}$ cups whole-wheat flour

$1/_{2}$ cup chilled bacon drippings

1 large egg

1 cup milk, or sufficient for processing, at room temperature

8-ounce package cream cheese, at room temperature

1. Position the rack in the center of the oven and preheat at 400°F. Lightly grease or use parchment paper to line two cookie sheets or baking trays.

2. Place the flour in a large bowl, and using a pastry blender or two knives, cut in the bacon drippings.

3. In a medium bowl, using a fork or wire whisk, beat the egg until foamy. Beat in the milk and cream cheese until smooth.

4. Using a large spoon, a spatula, or your hand, combine the two mixes, blending until the mixture pulls away from the sides of the bowl and forms a soft dough. If the mixture seems a little dry, add a little milk, a tablespoonful at a time.

5. Turn the dough onto a lightly floured flat surface, and knead 8 to 10 times. Pinch off pieces of the dough about the size of a small egg, and rolling between your hands, form into a rope about the size of a cigar. For smaller dogs, the thickness of the rope should be about the size of a pencil. Lay the rope on the prepared baking sheet, form into a ring, and pinch the ends together. Continue until all of the dough has been used.

6. Bake for 20 to 25 minutes or until the cookies appear very dry and the edges are light golden brown. Remove the trays from the oven and cool to room temperature. Turn off the oven.

7. When the cookies have cooled completely, put all of them on a single baking tray and return them to the cooling oven. Leave them undisturbed, without opening the oven door, for 8 to 16 hours.

PLEASE NOTE: Some dogs may be sensitive to dairy products.

WeStern Cow-dog BiSCUits

These cookies are thicker than most other cookies in this book. If you make them for smaller dogs, roll the dough out thinner (perhaps $1/2$ inch thick). Be sure to dry them according to directions.

3 to 3^{1}/$_2$ pounds (15 **cookies** per pound)

4 cups all-purpose flour

2 cups whole-wheat flour

1 cup yellow cornmeal

2 cups cracked wheat

$1/2$ cup nonfat dry milk

1 cup wheat germ

2 tablespoons brewer's yeast

1 large egg

$1/4$ cup melted vegetable shortening

$1/4$ cup honey

$2^1/2$ cups beef or chicken broth or drippings

1. Position the rack in the center of the oven and preheat at 400°F. Lightly grease or use parchment paper to line two cookie sheets or baking trays.

2. In a large bowl, using a fork or wire whisk, blend the two flours, cornmeal, cracked wheat, dry milk, wheat germ, and yeast.

3. In a medium bowl, using a wire whisk or electric mixer on MEDIUM speed, beat together the egg and shortening until smooth. Beat in the honey and broth.

4. Using a large spoon, a spatula, or your hand, combine the two mixes, blending until the mixture pulls away from the sides of the bowl and forms a soft dough. If the mixture seems a little dry, add a little broth, a tablespoonful at a time.

5. Turn the dough onto a lightly floured flat surface, and using a rolling pin, roll out to a thickness of $1/2$ to $3/4$ inch. Use a cookie cutter to cut out as many cookies as you can, reworking the scraps as you go. The dough will become stiff as it is reworked.

6. Place the cookies side by side on the prepared cookie sheets or baking trays. Bake for 25 to 30 minutes or until the cookies appear very dry and the edges are light golden brown. Remove the trays from the oven and cool to room temperature. Turn off the oven.

7. When the cookies have cooled completely, put all of them on a single baking tray and return them to the cooling oven. Leave them undisturbed, without opening the oven door, for 8 to 16 hours.

    PLEASE NOTE: Some dogs are allergic to corn-based products or sensitive to dairy products.

Bow-Wow's Birthday Balls

The flavor of the baby food should be enough to please any dog. I personally wanted to add more flavor for my dog, so I rolled each ball in the crumbled bacon. They didn't last any time at all in my pantry.

2 to 2^1/$_4$ pounds (30 balls per pound)

1 cup whole-wheat flour

1^1/$_2$ cups unbleached all-purpose flour

1^1/$_2$ teaspoons baking powder

^{1}/$_2$ cup vegetable shortening

2 large eggs

^{1}/$_4$ cup corn oil

4.5-ounce jar liver-flavored baby food

^{1}/$_2$ cup crumbled crisp cooked bacon

1. Position the rack in the center of the oven and preheat at 400°F. Lightly grease or use parchment paper to line two cookie sheets or baking trays.
2. In a large bowl, using a fork or wire whisk, blend the two flours and baking powder.
3. Using a pastry blender or two knives, cut in the shortening until the mixture resembles fine crumbs.
4. In a medium bowl, using a wire whisk or electric mixer on MEDIUM speed, beat the eggs until foamy. Beat in the oil and baby food until smooth.
5. Using a large spoon, a spatula, or your hand, combine the two mixes, blending until the mixture pulls away from the sides of the bowl and forms a soft dough. Turn the dough onto a lightly floured flat surface, and knead 8 to 10 times. Pinch off pieces of the dough and use your hands to form small balls about the size of walnuts. Roll each ball in the crumbled bacon and place them on the prepared baking trays about ^{1}/$_2$ inch apart.

6. Bake for 20 to 25 minutes or until the cookies appear very dry, have a light golden color, and the bacon appears as dark brown specks. Remove the trays from the oven and cool the cookies to room temperature. Turn off the oven.

7. When the cookies have cooled completely, put all of them on a single baking tray and return them to the cooling oven. Leave them undisturbed, without opening the oven door, for 8 to 16 hours.

PLEASE NOTE: Some dogs may be allergic to corn-based products.

Turkey & Cheese Treats

The processed cheese used as flavoring in these cookies is one of the most versatile flavoring products. It can be used with almost any poultry or meat. Dogs love it, and the smell and taste of the meat enhances the cookies.

3$\frac{1}{2}$ to 4 pounds (12 to 14 **cookies** per pound)

2 cups whole-wheat flour

$\frac{1}{2}$ cup graham flour

$\frac{1}{2}$ pound finely minced, cooked ground turkey

2 medium carrots, washed, peeled, and finely grated

3 tablespoons processed cheese spread

2 large eggs

2 tablespoons chicken broth, or sufficient for processing

1. Position the rack in the center of the oven and preheat at 400°F. Lightly grease or use parchment paper to line a cookie sheet or baking tray.

2. In a large bowl, using a fork or wire whisk, blend the two flours, turkey, carrots, and cheese. In a small bowl, using a fork or wire whisk, beat together the eggs and chicken broth.

3. Using a fork, make an indentation in the center of the dry mix and add the egg mixture.

4. Using a large spoon, a spatula, or your hand, blend until the mixture pulls away from the sides of the bowl and forms a soft dough. If the mixture seems a little dry, add a little broth, a tablespoonful at a time.

5. Turn the dough onto a lightly floured flat surface, and using a rolling pin, roll out to $1/4$ inch thick. Use a $1^1/2$-inch round cookie cutter to cut out as many cookies as you can, reworking the scraps as you go. The dough will become stiff as it is reworked.

6. Place the cookies side by side on the prepared cookie sheet or baking tray. Bake for 20 to 25 minutes or until the cookies appear very dry and the edges are light golden brown. Remove the trays from the oven and cool to room temperature. Turn off the oven.

7. When the cookies have cooled completely, put all of them on a single baking tray and return them to the cooling oven. Leave them undisturbed, without opening the oven door, for 8 to 16 hours.

PLEASE NOTE: Some dogs are sensitive to dairy products.

Sez-Me Treats

Although this recipe represents a small batch of cookies, it may seem to yield a lot more if you're preparing them for a small dog. Simply make the cookies smaller in size, or cut them into small squares instead of rounds. You'll then double the number of cookies per pound.

$3/4$ to 1 pound (24 **cookies** per pound)

1 cup whole-wheat flour

1 cup unbleached all-purpose flour

2 tablespoons toasted wheat germ

$1/2$ cup turbinado sugar

1 tablespoon desiccated liver

1 large egg

$1/2$ cup melted butter or margarine

$1/2$ cup beef or chicken broth, or sufficient for processing

$1/4$ cup sesame seeds

1. In a large bowl, using a fork or wire whisk, blend the two flours, wheat germ, sugar, and liver.

2. In a small bowl, using a fork or wire whisk, beat together the egg and butter, until smooth. Beat in the broth.

3. Using a fork, make an indentation in the center of the dry mix and add the egg mixture all at one time.

4. Using a large spoon, a spatula, or your hand, blend until the mixture pulls away from the sides of the bowl and forms a soft dough.

5. Turn the dough onto a lightly floured flat surface and knead 8 to 10 times. Cut the dough in half, form each half into a log about $1^1/2$ inches in diameter, and roll in sesame seeds. Wrap each log in waxed paper and chill in the refrigerator for about 4 hours or until ready to bake.

6. When you're ready to make the cookies, position the rack in the center of the oven and pre-heat at 350ºF. Lightly grease or use parchment paper to line a cookie sheet or baking tray.

7. Remove the log(s) from the refrigerator, and using a sharp knife, cut them into $1/2$-inch slices.

8. Place the slices side by side on the prepared baking sheet. Bake for about 15 to 20 minutes or until the cookies appear very dry and the edges are light golden brown. Remove the trays from the oven and cool to room temperature. Turn off the oven.

9. When the cookies have cooled completely, put all of them on a single baking tray and return them to the cooling oven. Leave them undisturbed, without opening the oven door, for 8 to 16 hours.

Fido's Egg dumplings

Not really a cookie, these little dumplings are usually something very special for dogs to eat. Once they have been cooked, they can be stored covered in the refrigerator, and a few of them can be given to the dog each day after a regular meal. Every dog that tasted them absolutely loved these dumplings.

24 dumplings

- **1 quart beef or chicken broth**
- **1 cup raw chicken livers**
- **2 large eggs, separated**
- **1 teaspoon freshly snipped parsley**
- **2 tablespoons melted butter or margarine**
- **$\frac{1}{2}$ cup whole-wheat flour**
- **$\frac{1}{2}$ cup graham flour**

1. In a large saucepan over MEDIUM LOW heat, warm the broth.
2. In a blender, process the chicken liver on HIGH until smooth. Beat in the egg yolks, parsley, and butter.
3. In a large bowl, using a fork or wire whisk, blend the two flours, and make an indentation in the center. Pour in the liver mixture, and using a large spoon, a spatula, or your hand, blend until the mixture pulls away from the sides of the bowl and a very soft, sticky dough forms.
4. Raise the heat on the broth, and when the mixture starts to boil, drop a heaping tea-spoonful of the mixture into the hot liquid. Cook for about 5 to 6 minutes, remove the dumplings from the broth, and cool on a wire rack until ready to serve to the dog.

   PLEASE NOTE: Cover and refrigerate any dumplings not served immediately.

Little Rye Loaves

I originally made these little loaves as a joke, never thinking a dog would go for them. Well, the joke turned out to be on me. The dogs absolutely love them. Because these are larger-than-normal treats, thoroughly dry them as noted in step 7. If you do not dry them, freeze the little loaves in separate plastic bags until you're ready to use them.

9 little **loaves** or **muffins**

3/4 cup all-purpose flour

1/2 cup whole-wheat flour

1 1/4 cups rye flour

2 teaspoons baking powder

3/4 cup nonfat dry milk

1 cup puréed raw chicken livers

1 large egg

1 1/2 cup chicken broth or drippings

3 tablespoons dark molasses

1. Position the rack in the center of the oven and preheat at 400°F. Lightly grease the bottom of each cup of a 9 x 3⅝ x 2½-inch muffin pan or little-loaf pan.

2. In a large bowl, using a fork or wire whisk, blend the three flours, baking powder, dry milk, and chicken.

3. In a medium bowl, using a wire whisk, or electric mixer on MEDIUM speed, beat the egg until foamy. Beat in the broth and molasses.

4. Using a large spoon or spatula, combine the two mixes, blending until the dry ingredients are just moistened. Drop 2 heaping tablespoonfuls of the mixture into the prepared baking pan, filling each cup about two-thirds full.

5. Bake for about 15 to 20 minutes or until the tops are a deep golden color and a wooden toothpick inserted into the muffins or loaves is removed clean.

6. Remove the pan from the oven and cool on a wire rack for 5 minutes before transferring the muffins or loaves to a serving plate. Turn off the oven. Remove the trays from the oven and cool to room temperature.

7. When the muffins have cooled completely, put all of them on a single baking tray and return them to the cooling oven. Leave them undisturbed, without opening the oven door, for 8 to 16 hours.

PLEASE NOTE: Some dogs may be sensitive to dairy products.

Bacon Drops

These drops are another great treat. The only problem is that they do not keep well. They should be used within a few days after baking. Otherwise, remove them from the oven, cool them completely, and wrap and freeze each one individually until you're ready to use them.

1 pound (98 **cookies** per pound)

2 cups all-purpose flour

3 teaspoons baking powder

$1/4$ cup nonfat dry milk

$1/4$ cup vegetable shortening

8 slices crisp cooked bacon, crumbled

1 cup chicken or beef broth, or sufficient for processing

1. Position the rack in the center of the oven and preheat at 400°F. Lightly grease or use parchment paper to line a cookie sheet or baking tray.

2. In a large bowl, using a fork, blend the flour, baking powder, and dry milk. Using a pastry blender or two knives, cut the shortening into the dry ingredients until the mixture resembles fine meal. Stir in the bacon. Make a small indentation in the center of the mixture, add the broth, and using a fork, work until the mixture forms a soft dough and pulls away from the sides of the bowl.

3. For each cookie, drop a teaspoonful of dough 1 inch apart onto the prepared baking sheet. Bake for about 10 to 12 minutes or until the tops of the cookies are light golden brown.

4. Remove from the oven, cool to room temperature, and refrigerate until ready to use.

PLEASE NOTE: Some dogs are sensitive to dairy products.

Liver doggie Biscuits

Have you ever sat at a breakfast table and had your dog, ever so friendly, sitting beside your chair and begging for something from your plate? Of course you have. We all have, and these cookies are a direct result of that intrusion. I keep one or two of these biscuits handy on the breakfast table. It allows me to give one to my favorite pet, and he'll never know he isn't getting something right off my plate.

12 biscuits

$1^3/_4$ cups all-purpose flour

2 teaspoons baking powder

6 tablespoons desiccated liver

1 tablespoon brewer's yeast

$1^3/_4$ cups beef or chicken broth, or sufficient for processing

1. Position the rack in the center of the oven and preheat at 375°F. Lightly grease or use parchment paper to line a cookie sheet or baking tray.
2. In a large bowl, using a fork or wire whisk, blend the flour, baking powder, liver, and yeast. Make an indentation in the center and pour in the broth, and using a large fork, a spatula, or your hand, blend until the mixture pulls away from the sides of the bowl and a very sticky, soft dough forms. If the mixture seems a little dry, add a little broth, a tablespoonful at a time.
3. Turn the dough onto a lightly floured flat surface, and using a rolling pin, roll out to $1/_2$ inch thick, and using a 1-inch round cookie cutter, cut out as many cookies as you can, reworking the scraps as you go. The dough will become stiff as it is reworked.
4. Place the cookies side by side on the prepared cookie sheet or baking tray. Bake for 18 to 22 minutes or until the cookies appear very dry and the edges are light golden brown. Remove the trays from the oven and cool to room temperature. Turn off the oven.
6. When the cookies have cooled completely, put all of them on a single baking tray and return them to the cooling oven. Leave them undisturbed, without opening the oven door, for 8 to 16 hours.

Tegga's Bread

Keep little loaves (muffins) of this dog treat in a plastic bag when you go on a trip or vacation with your dog. They're small, easy to handle, and can be broken off if you don't have a knife.

9 little **loaves** or **muffins**

3 cups whole-wheat flour

$^{1}/_{2}$ cup desiccated liver

2 teaspoons baking powder

1 tablespoon desiccated bone meal

$^{1}/_{2}$ cup finely grated fresh cheese

2 large eggs

$^{1}/_{4}$ cup canola oil

$1^{1}/_{2}$ cups beef or chicken broth, or sufficient for processing

1. Position the rack in the center of the oven and preheat at 375°F. Lightly grease each cup of a 9 x $3^{5}/_{8}$ x $2^{1}/_{2}$-inch muffin pan or little-loaf pan.
2. In a large bowl, using a fork or wire whisk, blend the flour, liver, baking powder, bone meal, and cheese.
3. In a medium bowl, using a wire whisk or electric mixer on MEDIUM speed, beat together the eggs, oil, and broth.
4. Using a large spoon, a spatula, or your hands, combine the two mixes, blending until the mixture pulls away from the sides of the bowl and a very sticky, soft dough forms.
5. Drop 2 heaping tablespoonfuls of the mixture into the cups of the prepared baking pan. Bake for about 20 to 25 minutes or until the tops are a golden brown color and a wooden toothpick inserted into them is removed clean. Turn off the oven.
6. Remove the pan from the oven and cool on a wire rack for 10 minutes before removing the muffins from the pan. Cool completely and wrap individually with waxed paper, and store in the refrigerator until ready to use. Or air-dry them in a cooling oven for 8 hours or overnight.

Value Cookies

These cookies contain lots of vitamins and minerals that are good for your dog. They're easy to make as cookies or bars.

1 to 1½ pounds (142 cookies per pound)

2 cups Bisquick® mix

½ cup desiccated liver

2 cups cottage cheese

½ cup canola oil

1 cup beef broth, or sufficient for processing

1. Position the rack in the center of the oven and preheat at 350°F. Lightly grease or use parchment paper to line two cookie sheets or baking trays.
2. In a large bowl, using a fork or wire whisk, blend the Bisquick and liver.
3. In a medium bowl, using a wire whisk or electric mixer on MEDIUM speed, beat together the cheese, oil, and broth.
4. Using a large spoon, a spatula, or your hands, combine the two mixes, blending until the mixture pulls away from the sides of the bowl and forms a soft dough.
5. Turn the dough onto a lightly floured flat surface, and using a rolling pin, roll out to ¼ inch thick. Using a 1-inch round cookie cutter, cut out as many cookies as you can, reworking the scraps as you go. The dough will become stiff as it is reworked.
6. Place the cookies side by side on the prepared cookie sheets or baking trays. Bake for 15 to 20 minutes or until the cookies appear very dry and the edges are light golden brown. Remove the trays from the oven and cool to room temperature. Turn off the oven.
7. When the cookies have cooled completely, put all of them on a single baking tray and return them to the cooling oven. Leave them undisturbed, without opening the oven door, for 8 to 16 hours.

ALTERNATE METHOD: Prepare as directed in steps 1 to 5. Roll out the dough to fit into a lightly greased jelly-roll pan, and bake for 15 to 20 minutes or until the top is a golden brown color. Remove from the oven and cool in the pan on a wire rack to room temperature. Turn off the oven.

Return to the oven and leave undisturbed for 8 to 10 hours, or overnight. Remove from the pan, and crumble into kibble-size bits. Feed as a treat as desired.

The world's Most Perfect dog Treat

The perfect treat is one your beloved dog, with his tail wagging, asks for at your feet, and enjoys with relish. These treats will be perfect if your pet does not have an allergy to any of these ingredients.

2 to 2½ pounds (98 **cookies** per pound)

4 cups whole-wheat flour

½ cup desiccated liver

¼ cup brewer's yeast

¼ cup desiccated bone meal

3 large eggs

¾ cup beef broth, or sufficient for processing

1. Position the rack in the center of the oven and preheat at 375°F. Have two ungreased cookie sheets or baking trays ready.

2. In a large bowl, using a fork or wire whisk blend the flour, liver, yeast, and bone meal.

3. In a medium bowl, using a wire whisk, or electric mixer on MEDIUM speed, beat the eggs and $\frac{1}{2}$ cup beef broth together until smooth. Beat in the remaining broth.

4. Using a large spoon, a spatula, or your hand, combine the two mixes, blending until a soft dough forms and pulls away from the sides of the bowl. If the mixture seems a little dry, add a little more broth, a tablespoonful at a time.

5. Turn the dough onto a lightly floured flat surface, and using a rolling pin, roll out to $\frac{1}{4}$ inch thick. Use a $1\frac{1}{2}$-inch round cookie cutter to cut out as many cookies as you can, reworking the scraps as you go. The dough will become stiff as it is reworked.

6. Place the cookies side by side on the prepared cookie sheets or baking trays. Bake for 18 to 20 minutes or until the cookies appear very dry and the edges are light golden brown. Remove the trays from the oven and cool to room temperature. Turn off the oven.

7. When the cookies have cooled completely, put all of them on a single baking tray and return them to the cooling oven. Leave them undisturbed, without opening the oven door, for 8 to 16 hours.

Three-grain doggie Bread

Although any of the treats in this book can be fed to a dog of any size, some treats are best suited to large dogs and some to small dogs. This doggie bread happens to be one of those best suited to the larger dog breeds.

6 to 8 little **loaves** or **muffins**

1 cup graham flour

1 cup rye flour

1 cup yellow cornmeal

$\frac{1}{4}$ cup desiccated liver

$^1/_2$ cup desiccated bone meal

2 teaspoons baking powder

1 large egg

$^1/_4$ cup molasses

$1^3/_4$ cups beef broth, or sufficient for processing

1. Position the rack in the center of the oven and preheat at 375°F. Lightly grease a 9 x 3$^5/_8$ x 2$^1/_2$-inch muffin pan or little-loaf pan.
2. In a large bowl, using a fork or wire whisk, blend the graham flour, rye flour, cornmeal, liver, bone meal, and baking powder.
3. In a medium bowl, using a wire whisk or electric mixer on MEDIUM speed, beat together the egg, molasses, and broth.
4. Using a large spoon, a spatula, or your hand, combine the two mixes, blending until the dry ingredients are just moistened. Drop 3 tablespoonfuls of the mixture into the prepared baking pan. Bake for about 15 to 20 minutes or until they are golden brown and a wooden toothpick inserted into the little muffins is removed clean.
5. Remove the pan from the oven and cool on a wire rack for 10 to 15 minutes before transferring the muffins to the wire rack to cool completely. Turn off the oven.
6. When the muffins have cooled completely, put all of them on a single baking tray and return them to the cooling oven. Leave them undisturbed, without opening the oven door, for 8 to 16 hours.

PLEASE NOTE: Some dogs may be allergic to corn-based products.

doggies Love Shortenin' Bread

Some veterinarians and animal nutritionists believe that pork fat is the best fat you can feed a dog. Here we have added pork fat not only to induce your dogs to eat the treats, but because it is, some folks believe, good for them.

8 to 10 little **loaves** or **muffins**

1 cup yellow corn flour

¾ cup whole-wheat flour

½ cup bulgur wheat

1½ teaspoons baking powder

1 cup sour cream

1 cup salt pork, rendered and finely chopped

¼ cup melted pork fat from salt pork

1. Position the rack in the center of the oven and preheat at 375°F. Lightly grease a 9 x 3⅝ x 2½-inch muffin pan or little-loaf pan.

2. In a large bowl, using a fork or wire whisk, blend the corn flour, whole-wheat flour, bulgur wheat, and baking powder.

3. In a medium bowl, using a wire whisk or electric mixer on MEDIUM speed, beat the sour cream until softened and smooth. Beat in the pork and fat.

4. Using a large spoon, a spatula, or your hand, combine the two mixes, blending until the dry ingredients are just moistened.

5. Drop 3 heaping tablespoonfuls of the mixture into the cups of the prepared baking pan. Bake for about 15 to 20 minutes or until a golden brown color and a wooden toothpick inserted into the muffins is removed clean.

6. Remove the pan from the oven and cool on a wire rack for 10 to 15 minutes before transferring the muffins or little loaves to the wire rack to cool completely. Drying these muffins or little loaves is not recommended.

WARNING: Pork fat will turn rancid quickly if not kept refrigerated.

PLEASE NOTE: Some dogs may be allergic to corn-based products or sensitive to dairy products.

Poochie Little Loaves

Most loaf treats were designed for people who like to take their dogs with them when traveling. These treats tempt the vacationing dog with the sweet flavor of carrots.

4 to 6 small **loaves** or **muffins**

2 cups whole-wheat flour

2 teaspoons baking powder

1 cup finely grated carrots

2 large eggs

$^1/_4$ cup chicken livers

$^3/_4$ cup canola oil or corn oil

1. Position the rack in the center of the oven and preheat at 375°F. Lightly grease a 9 x 3 $^5/_8$ x 2 $^1/_2$-inch muffin pan or little-loaf pan.
2. In a large bowl, using a fork or wire whisk, blend the flour, baking powder, and carrots.
3. In a medium bowl, using a wire whisk or electric mixer on MEDIUM speed, beat the eggs thick and light-colored. Beat in the chicken livers and oil.
4. Using a large spoon, a spatula, or your hand, combine the two mixes, blending until the dry ingredients are just moistened.
5. Drop 3 heaping tablespoonfuls of the mixture into the cups of the prepared baking pan. Bake for about 15 to 20 minutes or until they are golden brown and a wooden tooth-pick inserted into the muffins or little loaves is removed clean.
5. Remove the pan from the oven and cool on a wire rack for 10 to 15 minutes before transferring the muffins to the wire rack to cool completely. Turn off the oven.
6. After the muffins are at room temperature, place them on a cookie sheet, and return them to the cooling oven for 8 to 12 hours to dry.

   PLEASE NOTE: Some dogs may be allergic to corn-based products.

Love 'em Honey Bread

Fact: Dogs love sweet things. Unfortunately, there are very few sweet things that we can give them with confidence. Here I have chosen to use honey; it's natural and shouldn't hurt them.

6 little **loaves** or **muffins**

MUFFINS

> 2 cups whole-wheat flour
>
> $2^1/_2$ teaspoons baking powder
>
> 2 large eggs
>
> 1 cup sour cream or unflavored yogurt
>
> $^1/_4$ cup warm honey

CHICKEN GLAZE (TOPPING)

> $^1/_2$ cup chicken broth
>
> 1 package unflavored gelatin

1. Position the rack in the center of the oven and preheat at 375°F. Lightly grease a 9 x 3 $^5/_8$ x 2$^1/_2$-inch muffin pan or 6 little-loaf pans.

2. In a large bowl, using a fork or wire whisk, blend the flour and baking powder.

3. In a medium bowl, using a wire whisk or electric mixer on MEDIUM speed, beat the eggs until thick and light-colored. Beat in the sour cream and honey.

4. Using a large spoon, a spatula, or your hand, combine the two mixes, sour cream, and honey. Drop 3 heaping tablespoonfuls of the mixture into the cups of the prepared baking pan. Bake for about 15 to 20 minutes or until they are golden brown and a wooden toothpick inserted into the muffins or little loaves is removed clean.

5. Remove the pan from the oven and cool on a wire rack for 10 to 15 minutes before transferring the muffins to the wire rack to cool completely. Brush with the chicken glaze, and set aside to dry. Turn off the oven.

6. To make the chicken glaze, pour $^1/_2$ cup boiling chicken broth in a cup, and stir in one envelope of unflavored gelatin until dissolved.

7. Place the cooled muffins on a cookie sheet and return them to the oven, with the heat off, and leave them undisturbed for 8 to 12 hours.

COOKING NOTE: You can make a beef glaze; just substitute beef broth for the chicken broth. Brush either glaze on these or other cookies and treats.

PLEASE NOTE: Some dogs may be sensitive to dairy products.

Abtu's Pigglys

This recipe was created in memory of the first Basenji I ever owned, Abtu Teti Hotep. All my dogs bear an ancient Egyptian name. I remember Abtu with joy and sadness and honor him with these cookies.

1 to 1½ pound (52 **cookies** per pound)

2 cups whole-wheat flour

1 tablespoon brewer's yeast

¼ cup desiccated bone meal

½ cup cooked rice

½ cup beef or chicken broth, or sufficient for processing

½ pound salt pork, rendered and finely chopped

1. Position the rack in the center of the oven and preheat at 400°F. Lightly grease or use parchment paper to line a cookie sheet or baking tray.

2. In a large bowl, using a fork or wire whisk, blend the flour, yeast, and bone meal.

3. In a small bowl, using an electric mixer on HIGH speed, beat together the rice, broth, and salt pork.

4. Using a fork, make an indentation in the center of the dry mix and add the rice mixture.

5. Using a large spoon, a spatula, or your hand, blend until the mixture pulls away from the sides of the bowl and forms a soft dough. If the mixture seems a little dry, add a little broth, a tablespoonful at a time.

6. Turn the dough onto a lightly floured flat surface, and using a rolling pin, roll out to $1/4$ inch thick. Use a $1^1/_2$-inch round cookie cutter to cut out as many cookies as you can, reworking the scraps as you go. The dough will become stiff as it is reworked.

7. Place the cookies side by side on the prepared cookie sheet or baking tray. Bake for 20 to 25 minutes or until the cookies appear very dry and the edges are light golden brown. Remove the trays from the oven and cool to room temperature. Turn off the oven.

8. When the cookies have cooled completely, put all of them on a single baking tray and return them to the cooling oven. Leave them undisturbed, without opening the oven door, for 8 to 16 hours.

Gregg's Special dog Food

This book contains recipes for dog biscuits and cookies rather than main-meal dog chow. A recipe book on dog chow is rightly reserved for a dog nutritionist. The dog-cookie recipes in this book are nutritious and serve as supplements for your dog's diet. Many people have asked what I serve my dogs; here's one of the healthful meals I've prepared. I've also noted through the years that many individual dogs have allergies to certain foods, such as corn-based products. I avoid feeding my dogs corn in everyday meals.

4 to 5 pounds

1 to 1$^1/_2$ pounds freshly ground lamb
1 to 2 small cloves of garlic, minced
2 tablespoons brewer's yeast

1 cup brown rice

$1/2$ cup wild rice

2 small potatoes, diced

3 fresh spinach leaves, finely chopped

3 medium carrots, pared and finely chopped

1. In a Crock-Pot®, electric casserole, heavy-duty saucepan, or kettle, on MEDIUM-LOW heat, bring about $1/2$ gallon (4 cups) of water to a boil.

2. In a large skillet over a MEDIUM-HOT heat, sauté the lamb until well browned and stir into the water in the Crock-Pot.

3. In the same skillet, quickly sauté the garlic until tender. Add 2 tablespoons of the hot liquid from the Crock-Pot to the garlic, stirring briefly. Then pour the garlic and its liquid into the Crock-Pot.

4. Add all of the remaining ingredients and cook in the Crock-Pot slowly on LOW for 4 to 6 hours.

5. Remove from the heat, cool to room temperature, and refrigerate for 2 to 4 hours.

6. When ready, using a measuring cup, place 1 full cup of the mixture into a zipper type of plastic bag, and seal and freeze until ready to use. Be sure to label and date the bag. Feed your dog as usual.

PLEASE NOTE: Some dogs may be allergic to garlic.

doggie Pasta

This is my latest creation. I bought a pasta machine for just the purpose of creating my own doggie pasta. If you have a pasta machine and want to make the ultimate dog treat, this is it. If you don't have a pasta machine, you can easily modify this recipe. Like all recipes in this book, this one is simple, and ingredients can be found in health-food stores.

1 pound uncooked pasta

$1^2/_3$ cups plus 3 teaspoons all-purpose flour

1 tablespoon desiccated liver

1 teaspoon nutritional yeast

1 tablespoon whey powder or nonfat dry milk

1 tablespoon bone meal

1 large egg, beaten

1 tablespoon canola oil

8 tablespoons water or chicken bouillon

woof

1. In a bowl, combine the flour, liver, yeast, whey powder, and bone meal. Blend thoroughly.
3. In a second bowl, beat together the egg, oil, and water.
3. Process through the pasta machine according to the manufacturer's directions.
4. In a large saucepan bring about 4 quarts of water to a rolling boil and immediately cook the pasta al dente. Drain and do not rinse. Cool to room temperature and serve. The cooked pasta may also be stored for a day or two in a refrigerator.

INDEX of Doggie Treats

A

Abtu's Pigglys, 123
Abu's Best, 38
Animal-Shelter Puppy Treats, 42
Apit's Love Cookies, 43

B

Bacon & Liver Treats, 102
Bacon Drops, 113
Beef-Flavored Canine Cookies, 77
Beef Your Baby Treats, 61
Bow-Wow's Birthday Balls, 106

C

Canine Cookies, 97
Carrot & Cheese Dog Treats, 54
Cheese Biscuits, 82
Cheesy-Cheese Dog Treats, 70
Cheesy Rings, 103

Chick-a-Dee Dog Biscuits, 80
Chicken & Cheese Treats, 86
Chicken Biscuits, 93
Chicken-Gizzard Treats, 88
Chicken-Liver Treats, 96
Chickie Do's, 85
Coming-through-the-Rye Treats, 58
Corn-Doggie Dogs, 52

D

Dobis, 34
Dobis Variations, 35
Dog Sticks, 101
Doggie Balls, 50
Doggie Nibble Bars, 81
Doggie Oatmeal Cookies, 66
Doggie Pasta, 126
Doggie Stocking Stuffers, 74
Doggies Love Shortenin' Bread, 120
Dog's Soupy Treats, 84

E

Easy Doggie Strips, 91
Eggs, Liver & Rice Cookies, 68

F

Familiar Dog Treats, 89
Fido's Egg Dumplings, 110
15-Minute Dog Cookies, 100
Flea-Away Biscuits, 60

G

Garlic Nugget Balls, 51
Green & Gold Doggie Cookies, 64
Gregg's Special Dog Food, 124

H

Healthy Liver Treats, 67
Honey-Love Biscuits, 44

L

Lamb Cookies, 47
Lazy Man's Dog Cookies, 65
Little Liver Squares, 76
Little Rye Loaves, 111
Liver & Cheese Cookies, 62
Liver Doggie Biscuits, 114
Liver Treats, 56
Love 'em Honey Bread, 122

M

Manu's Favorite Lamb Treats, 46
Meat & Garlic Cookies, 48
Metric Equivalents, 26
Min-Tari's Carrot Cookies, 39

N

Nefer's Nuggets, 36

O

Oatmeal Cookies with Peanut Butter, 71

P

Poochie Little Loaves, 121

Q

Quickie Turkey Dog Treats, 55

S

Sez-Me Treats, 108
Simplest Dog Biscuits, 94
Sweet Seeds Dog Treats, 73

T

Tegga's Bread, 115
Tegga's Terrific Treats, 40
Three-Grain Doggie Bread, 118
Tuna Treats, 57
Turkey & Cheese Treats, 107

V

Value Cookies, 116
Vegetable-Flavored Doggie Cookies, 98

W

Western Buckwheat Dog Biscuits, 78
Western Cow-Dog Biscuits, 104
Woof Balls, 92
World's Most Perfect Dog Treat, The, 117